Do it with an
Architect

'Twas on a Monday evening the architect did call,
She said that we should open plan, remove the middle wall,
A simple beam would do the trick, and we need have no fear,
She suggested the name of a structural engineer.
Oh, it all makes work for professionals to do...

'Twas on a Tuesday evening the engineer came round,
He said we'd need new foundations dug well below the ground,
Exactly how much it would cost he really didn't know,
Any quantity surveyor could estimate it, though.
Oh, it all makes work for professionals to do...

'Twas on a Wednesday evening the QS stopped by,
He asked us a lot of questions like how and where and why,
And would we need to reroute the heating and the power,
A good services consultant could tell us in an hour.
Oh, it all makes work for professionals to do...

'Twas on a Thursday evening the services man came,
He said our boiler was too small, it really was a shame,
We'd need new radiators and our lights were not in line,
It was something that a specialist in lighting could design.
Oh, it all makes work for professionals to do...

'Twas on a Friday evening the lights man did arrive,
Our pendants were much too weak and our spots were all alive,
He could suggest a layout so that everyone could see,
But then of course, the architect would first have to agree.
Oh, it all makes work for professionals to do...

On Saturday and Sunday they do no work at all,
So 'twas on a Monday evening the architect did call...

Louis Hellman
(with apologies to Flanders & Swann)

Do it with an
Architect

How to survive refurbishing your home

Barbara Weiss
Louis Hellman

MITCHELL BEAZLEY in association with RIBA Publications

To all our clients,
past and future

Do it with an Architect
How to survive refurbishing your home
by **Barbara Weiss** and **Louis Hellman**

First published in Great Britain in 1999 by Mitchell Beazley,
an imprint of Octopus Publishing Group Ltd, 2–4 Heron Quays,
London E14 4JP

RIBA Publications' consultant **Sarah Lupton**
Authors' consultant **Dr David Chappell**

Executive Editor **Alison Starling**
Executive Art Editor **Vivienne Brar**
Senior Editor **Anthea Snow**
Editor **Kirsty Seymour-Ure**
Designer **Clare Sheddon**
Illustrator **Stefan Chabluk**
Picture Research **Jenny Faithfull**, **Helen Stallion**
Production **Rachel Staveley**
Indexer **Sue Farr**

ISBN 1 84000 194 1

A CIP record for this book is available from the British Library

Set in Adobe Garamond and Rotis
Colour reproduction by Eray Scan Pte Ltd
Produced by Toppan Printing Co., (HK) Ltd.
Printed and bound in China

Contents

AS SEEN BY THE PUBLIC...

BY THE CLIENT...

BY THE QUANTITY SURVEYOR...

BY THE PLANNING OFFICER...

BY THE BUILDER...

AND BY HIMSELF

THE IMAGE OF THE ARCHITECT

Introduction

On the rare occasions that an architect features in drama, it is usually as the tortured or high-powered genius – Gary Cooper in *The Fountainhead*, Paul Newman in *The Towering Inferno* or Brian Dennehy in *The Belly of an Architect*. By contrast, in the 1948 comedy *Mr Blandings Builds his Dream House*, starring Cary Grant and Myrna Loy, the architect is seen, briefly, in his (it's always his) role as consultant designer to an "ordinary" family who intend to build a new house for themselves. The results are hilarious, with the architect portrayed not as a romantic hero but as a world-weary pawn in the whole farcical process.

The majority of architects in the UK run small practices and work in the domestic field, more often than not revamping and extending old properties for family clients. Despite the interventions of the Prince of Wales there seems to be widespread ignorance or misconceptions regarding the work of such architects, and of its value and importance to society. There are innumerable soaps, dramas and comedies on television centred on the work of other professions such as doctors, nurses, vets, lawyers, the police and journalists – but nothing to do with architects. Yet their day-to-day work and their contact with clients, builders and officialdom are no less rich or filled with human drama. There must be room at least for a female architect–private detective who solves crimes through her knowledge of the way buildings function: "Elementary, my dear Wattage, the thief clearly entered through that air-conditioning duct!"

Despite the public's misconceptions as far as the work of the "GP" architect is concerned, a great many people in the course of their lives become involved in major house refurbishment, with or without the services of an architect, sometimes "doing it themselves". Expenditure on small-scale domestic works in the UK amounts to some £9 billion per annum (E & FN Spon, *Home Improvement Price Book*), involving probably around 200,000 households. There are no statistics that show how many of these projects go wrong in terms of cost and time overruns, but the world of small building works is fraught with such problems. The public's perception of this world is coloured by endless horror stories circulated by unhappy house owners who have ventured into the minefield alone, unprepared and ill-equipped. People too often embark on alterations to their homes with no professional advice and with only vague ideas regarding what they want to achieve, dishing out "money up front" to builders they know nothing about and with no written agreement or contract.

Admittedly, refurbishing a home is not for the fainthearted. It may be compared to a stressful but ultimately satisfying life event, such as having a baby: a long, complicated process involving many participants, including the parents (the owners), the doctors (the architects and consultants) and a whole team of midwives (the builders). It should be a very positive voyage of discovery, but the level of commitment demanded must be appreciated. A considerable amount of time and patience is required, as the process cannot be rushed. Like having children, a refurbishment involves having to make constant choices – financial, aesthetic and practical – and this can often lead to conflict; but the process should be fun, not a continual compromise with someone else's wishes.

Developing a custom-made home offers a far more fulfilling experience and sense of achievement than adopting someone else's ready-made product, and should be profitable in the long run if properly designed and planned in advance. From the authors' extensive experience in the field and in dealing with individual home owners, it is clear that all parties involved, not only the clients, benefit from professional advice and guidance from the word go. The authors make no apology for extolling the qualities of architects as the only professionals in the construction industry who are trained in both the design and the monitoring of the building operation, being at the same time composers and conductors of the "frozen music" of architecture.

This step-by-step guide takes you through the process of altering your home in a practical and informative way, aiming to generate sufficient understanding of the various stages to allow you to reach your own conclusions and to participate actively and creatively in the whole process.

Getting started

Assessing your needs
Why employ an architect
Choosing your architect
Fees and expenses

Assessing your needs

The adventure begins

So you have fallen in love with a house, made an offer and bought it; now you want to alter and refurbish it so that it is tailored to your particular needs. Or perhaps you have decided that it is time for a change, or your family circumstances have altered, or everything is wearing out, and you want to remodel your house or flat, or a particular part of it. How to proceed?

Well, you could ask a builder or a surveyor for advice, although this would be a bit like asking a frame-maker to paint you a picture or a pharmacist to carry out heart surgery. Or you could consult a professional trained in all aspects of design, building construction and planning and contractual law: an architect. This guide strongly advocates appointing an architect before making any commitments, for reasons that will become apparent.

The bottom line

Before appointing an architect it will save time if you can establish an overall budget. If you are intending to fund the work with an extension of your mortgage or through a bank loan you should discuss the details with the prospective lenders and agree an amount that you can afford in terms of repayments and interest. Once this has been defined your architect can work within your budget and help to avoid great disappointment if you find you cannot afford your ideal project. Note also that your design team as well as the builders will need stage payments during the contract, and so you should discuss with the lenders how the funds will be released.

ANY FUTURE CHANGES TO YOUR FAMILY COMPOSITION ?

Plan ahead

Spend some time thinking hard about the spatial characteristics of your house and garden, which rooms get the sun and when, whether some rooms are dark or cold, if any bedrooms are disturbed by noise from neighbours or the street, and so on. Identify wasted or awkward space and storage difficulties. Make a list of requirements to meet your new needs. Think long term – how many years you intend to live in the property, whether your family is likely to expand or contract, whether your lifestyle is going to change dramatically over the next few years because of work, change in family composition, ageing, or having to accommodate elderly parents. Draw up a list of essential priorities. Consider organizing a phased development if you cannot afford everything you want immediately.

Value judgments

If you have just bought your property, you will most likely have had a survey carried out prior to the purchase. Make sure that all repairs and recommendations listed by the surveyor are passed on to your architect to be included in your budget. If you do not have a written survey, your architect can inspect the house and advise on repairs. He or she will probably recommend that an appropriate contingency sum is set aside for works yet to be identified (approximately 20 per cent of value of works). It is important to ensure that the fabric of your house (roof, walls, windows) is in good condition, and all the services (wiring, heating, plumbing), before leaping into glamorous extensions

Typical project cost breakdown

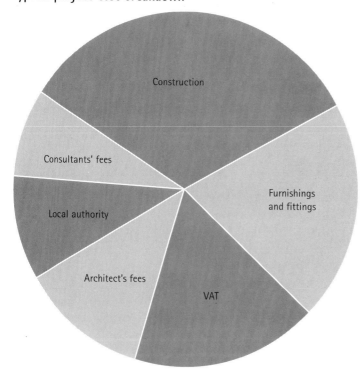

Construction

Consultants' fees

Furnishings and fittings

Local authority

Architect's fees

VAT

or interiors. When budgeting, remember that the building
contract does not normally include furnishings and loose fittings,
so include a sum for curtains, blinds, carpets, lampshades and
furniture generally.

Consult local estate agents regarding the value of your
house as it is now and as it would be after any conversions.
Some improvements add to the value of property, some do not.
Increasing the number of bedrooms or bathrooms, and improving
kitchens and lighting, make your house more desirable. Adding
gold taps or cladding a suburban semi-detached in marble will
not pay off in the long run.

Street legal

In trying to establish the feasibility of your proposed works, it
can be helpful to telephone your council office's planning
department and discuss your general intentions with a duty
planning officer. Do you live in a listed building or in a
Conservation Area? What is the council's attitude to extensions,
loft conversions, changes to the elevations or parking? Once
appointed, your architect will negotiate with the planners as a first
priority, but it will save time if you have sounded them out on any
possible general restrictions beforehand. However, avoid becoming
too specific or giving your address, as you do not want to risk
prejudicing your architect's future negotiations with the planners.

At the planning office you can sometimes pick up leaflets
with design guidelines for your area. Ask for copies of these, as
they will certainly provide useful information for your architect.

If you have newly acquired your property, your solicitor
should have made searches regarding any long-term development
policy plans for your area. Your solicitor should also have advised

Typical programme for a contract of approx. £80,000

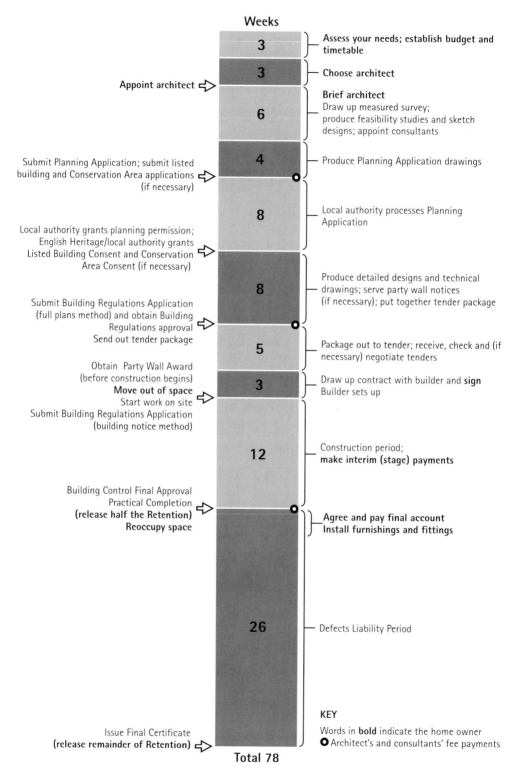

Weeks

3 — Assess your needs; establish budget and timetable

3 — Choose architect

Appoint architect ⇨

6 — **Brief architect**
Draw up measured survey;
produce feasibility studies and sketch
designs; appoint consultants

Submit Planning Application; submit listed
building and Conservation Area applications ⇨
(if necessary)

4 — Produce Planning Application drawings

8 — Local authority processes Planning Application

Local authority grants planning permission;
English Heritage/local authority grants
Listed Building Consent and Conservation ⇨
Area Consent (if necessary)

8 — Produce detailed designs and technical drawings; serve party wall notices (if necessary); put together tender package

Submit Building Regulations Application
(full plans method) and obtain Building
Regulations approval ⇨
Send out tender package

5 — Package out to tender; receive, check and (if necessary) negotiate tenders

Obtain Party Wall Award
(before construction begins)
Move out of space ⇨

3 — Draw up contract with builder and **sign** Builder sets up

Start work on site
Submit Building Regulations Application
(building notice method)

12 — Construction period; **make interim (stage) payments**

Building Control Final Approval
Practical Completion
(release half the Retention) ⇨
Reoccupy space

Agree and pay final account
Install furnishings and fittings

26 — Defects Liability Period

KEY

Issue Final Certificate
(release remainder of Retention) ⇨

Words in **bold** indicate the home owner
⭘ Architect's and consultants' fee payments

Total 78

you as to whether there are any restrictive covenants in your titles or leases that prevent you from, say, having an office within a residential area or carrying out certain types of work, and discussed with you any other legal issues that might affect your works, such as easements over your land or rights of light.

Your move

If you are embarking on substantial works that will affect several rooms at once, it is advisable to budget for alternative accommodation during the course of the refurbishment works. Attempting to live on a building site, as some people do, is not a good idea. It is dirty, noisy, dangerous and generally stress-inducing, particularly if there are small children around. The cost of the work and the time it takes will inevitably be much greater if the builders have to work round you. Discuss the options with your architect and ask for advice.

Well before any sort of building work starts, try to get on friendly terms with your neighbours, discuss your general plans and keep them informed as to what might be involved, since they may be affected by noise, dirt and builders' lorries. If they have no objections after informal discussions, confirm your intentions in writing. Attitudes can change drastically once the work commences, so it is useful to start off on the right foot, with clear lines of communication.

Why employ an architect

What is an architect?

There seems to be a general confusion as to what architects do, who they are and what their contribution is. In the UK, training takes seven years before full qualification and equips an architect to cope with the complex and wide-ranging facets of designing and building buildings, or parts of buildings. The architect needs to have some familiarity with a great many areas of activity, from aesthetics to technology, contractual law to environmental psychology, soil mechanics to philosophy, geography to human management, energy conservation to interior design. Even on a relatively small project, such as a rear kitchen extension, the architect is likely to have to apply a knowledge of many of these areas.

A myth is as good as a mile

Nonetheless, many myths abound. Architects only design the outsides of buildings. They are airy-fairy and impractical. They will spend their client's money on unnecessary fripperies. Architects are a waste of money: builders will do the same thing for free. Architects will force people to have weird designs they do not want; and so on and so on. Perhaps there are a few architects who fit the myths, but the majority provide a valuable service on many levels of expertise and experience.

Unlike doctors or lawyers, architects are in direct competition with other professions, such as surveyors, builders or project managers (usually surveyors), all of whom may offer "design" services. Of course only registered architects may use the word "architect" after their names, but there are ways around this, for example using deliberately ambiguous descriptions such as "architectural designer" or "building designer". Beware of such titles, since their holders probably have no architectural qualifications and will not be registered architects. The idea that anybody can design a building is perhaps characteristic of the British love of the amateur – although this does not usually extend to brain surgery or aviation. Building design today can be an equally complex procedure and is best handled by those who are experienced and professionally qualified.

Small can be beautiful

People may know the big star names
of architects who design Millennium
Domes or international airports,
although they are rarely familiar with
the work and identity of the majority
of architects who labour away in
smaller practices. The latter's projects
might be less well known to the
general public, but the architectural
quality of these schemes is often
superior to that of more commercial
developments. The domestic market – be it new-build,
conversions or extensions to existing buildings – often constitutes
the bread and butter of smaller practices, as projects of this scale
are, in architectural terms, labour intensive and therefore difficult
to sustain for large offices with high overheads.

The orchestrator

The architect may be compared both to the composer of the
music and to the conductor of an orchestra. Architectural plans
are like music scores and, in a similar fashion, are instantly
interpreted on many levels by those who can read them. Although
to the layperson they might appear to be beautiful in themselves,
their function is to be blueprints for the performance – the
building. Architecture is the concept, the theme and variations,
first in the architect's mind, then on paper and finally realized
through the instruments – the building materials. It is the
architect's responsibility to coordinate the tempo and melody
produced by all the many instrumentalists involved in the piece:

the engineers, the planners, the cost consultants, the contractors and so on. All of these performers are dependent on instructions and information provided to them by the architect, who acts as the single point of contact between them and the client.

The enabler

All building projects, large or small, involve a highly complex process which includes design, dealing with Planning and Building Control (see pp.45–6) and other statutory and legal issues, producing technical drawings, writing specifications (see pp.51–2), going out to competitive tender (see pp.50–53), construction and administration. The journey is fraught with pitfalls. A good architect will guide you through each stage, taking the brunt of the organizational load and helping you at all times to make informed choices. Furthermore, proper design and planning will save money in the long run. The architect's experience in organizing the whole project from inception to completion helps to avoid unforeseen expenses. If required, the architect will liaise with a cost consultant; if not, he or she will be able to advise on costs and prices. The aim is to have everything in the building decided, specified and costed, down to the last nail, before work starts, so that nothing is left to chance and extras are kept to a minimum.

Ride those cowboys

Architects are likely to have a "stable" of regular competent builders they have worked with before. These builders will probably want to do a good job for you so that your architect will continue to consider them for future work. However, if you prefer to appoint builders not on the architect's list, the architect will check their references and the standards of their work and discuss their general performance with other architects or previous clients. It is in the architect's interest that the contractor selected is the most appropriate for the job in hand; the architect's experience will help you to appoint the right horse for the course.

Design of the times

No other member of the building industry has to cope with such a range of disciplines. Builders build, surveyors survey, quantity surveyors monitor costs, building inspectors apply the regulations, fire officers ensure means of escape; the architect has to know about all these aspects and take the wider view. Most importantly, the architect is the only member of the building industry trained in all aspects of design, involving the strategic working out on paper of the concept and the careful resolution of the detail. Intelligent design is one of the most important aspects in any field of activity – and it saves money in the long run.

Design guide

Therefore, it must be stressed that one of the main reasons for employing an architect is his or her ability to design. This does not mean simply drawing seductive pictures, but rather guiding you through the whole process of investigating your needs and requirements, working closely with you, and consulting you and keeping you informed at every stage. An architect can be a good sounding board for your ideas and can help you think about your lifestyle and how it may be enhanced – or even changed.

Choosing your architect

Marriage guidance

The client/architect relationship is the key to a successful project. At the end of the ordeal your architect will know you incredibly well (better than would a psychoanalyst, it has been said) in terms of your aesthetic preferences, your lifestyle, the way you operate, and how you behave under stress. So you must be sure at the beginning of the project that your architect will be able to guide you with patience through the maze of operations,

will encourage you to express yourself, and will have the capacity to keep the momentum going and generally to communicate on your wavelength.

Each architectural practice is substantially different from the next, both stylistically and in the way it works. The emphasis of the specific interests of one practice can vary tremendously from that of another, from "green architecture" to conservation, or from the most recent design theories to community concerns.

When choosing whom to work with, aim at identifying a practice that shares your personal concerns.

Starting up

To kick off the process of selecting an architect you could start by looking through interior design or architectural magazines and marking the designs you like. You might also consult friends who have been through the same experience and ask for recommendations (or whom to avoid).

Another way is to approach the Client Advisory Service of the Royal Institute of British Architects (RIBA) and ask to see the portfolios of different practices who do the sort of work that will be involved in your project. You could also look at publications such as *New Architects: A Guide to Britain's Best Young Architectural*

Practices, (Architecture Foundation,1997), if you want a very modern design. These days many architects are creating their own web sites, which will allow you with little effort to view several illustrations of their work. The practice you select does not necessarily have to be local to your house, although it can be an advantage if your architect knows the planning officers in your area.

Do not:

- look through Yellow Pages with a pin
- go by word of mouth only
- ring up Uncle Fred who used to be a draughtsman with a local firm of builders

Shopping around

As architects now compete for work it is a good idea to interview several before making a final choice. This is the best way to ensure that you find an architect appropriate for your project and with whom you are compatible.

Think about gender issues and whether it will be easier for you to discuss design matters with a man or a woman. Or maybe it is irrelevant.

On the rare occasions when the scale and scope of the project justify it, you might consider running a mini-competition in which you invite ideas or sketches from three or four firms and choose a winner. If you are potentially interested in following this route, you should approach the RIBA to obtain its guidelines on competitions.

Auditions

At the initial meeting you should obtain information regarding:

- the size and composition of the practice
- the practice's previous experience in a similar scale of house refurbishment
- references from ex-clients
- insurance levels
- whom you will be dealing with on a day-by-day basis, whether senior partner or assistant architect
- the fee structure proposed (see pp.23–5)
- how expenses are charged (see p.26–7)
- how soon the practice could start on your project

At the same time inspect the architect's portfolio and ask lots of questions about the projects, what the costs were, whether they ran over budget and time, how long the design time was, whether there were any problems with the planners, whether the client was satisfied, and so on. Discuss client participation in design decision-making and how many people will be working on your project. The architect will also ask you questions, namely about your initial brief, budget forecast and time-scale, and will try to get a feeling for your personal taste, although, initially, you will be expected to keep a fairly open mind regarding your scheme.

In architecture, a wealth of academic qualifications and professional affiliations does not necessarily denote the best designer, still less the easiest person to work with. Architecture is fundamentally a practical art. It is most important, therefore, to follow your gut feeling about the qualities of the person with whom you will be spending many hours and to whom you will be entrusting a great deal of responsibility for your future home and financial outlay.

Check the product

Unlike, perhaps, doctors or lawyers whose services you have to take on trust, architects produce a tangible product. Their previous projects are there for you to inspect and judge. It is vital to empathize with your architect's design style, and it is not advisable to work with an architect who has difficulty in accommodating your taste, or whose tastes you do not share. So it is important that you ask the architects whom you have interviewed to arrange visits to a few of their built projects in order to establish that you are in sympathy with what you see. Imagine yourself living in these environments. Be critical!

Fees and expenses

Fee, fie, foe, fum

The subject of fees can be a tricky one for domestic clients. Refurbishing a house (or sometimes even just a single room) is a relatively large financial undertaking, and fees are invariably paid grudgingly, with a suspicion that the money would have been better spent on the building work. Owing to the public's general misconceptions about the role of architects, clients often do not appreciate until well into the project how much time and effort have gone into the job. Discussing and agreeing fees and what they are for is important for both parties at the start; the details of payment should be resolved as soon as you are ready to begin talking about design.

WE COULD HAVE HAD A SECOND BATHROOM FOR THAT!

Cut price, cut corners

It should be pointed out that small (up to £50,000) and medium-sized (up to £150,000) domestic work is generally not very lucrative for architects, particularly for those with larger offices and high overheads. This is because domestic work is particularly labour intensive and your architect can easily spend almost as much time on a small project as on one with a much larger budget. To date, the average domestic fee structure does not recognize this, and architects often end up with minimal returns

ER, LET'S GO INTO THE CONFERENCE AREA!

for their efforts. If your project falls within the small or medium budget category and you want to keep your fees low, it might be worth approaching a smaller practice with low overheads or a single practitioner. They will devote much personal attention to your scheme and might prove to be more flexible in terms of, for example, being available to meet you after normal working hours.

However, if you are set on a particular architect, perhaps because of a certain design style, or on a larger practice, you might have to agree to pay higher fees for their services. Besides enjoying the luxury of living in a home "signed" by the architect of your choice, by employing a better-known or a larger practice you might benefit from better office support and facilities, such as technical and samples libraries, smoother administration, and occasionally a variety of services under one roof.

Whatever your decision, beware of "cut-price" fees; these could lead to a rushed design phase, which might well end up costing you more in the long run, when you discover that what you are building does not match your expectations and that the contractor has not allowed for many items required.

Tender subjects

Before Margaret Thatcher, as prime minister, enforced competition for the professions, the RIBA operated a minimum and mandatory sliding scale of fees relating to a percentage of the overall cost of the works. Architects were not supposed to undercut this minimum. Now, while the RIBA still suggests fee guidelines and publishes a recommended percentage fee scale, all fees are open to negotiation and many new buildings are the subject of fee bidding, although for obvious reasons this is not the best method of selecting an architect. If you wanted your portrait painted you would not choose the cheapest artist but one whose works you were sympathetic with. It is possible, however, even in small domestic works, for you to ask several architects to quote fees, although, as you must ensure that they are all bidding on the same basis, you will need to submit a detailed schedule of the work to be undertaken. If you choose this route, you should allow a minimum of two weeks to interview the candidates and familiarize them with your site

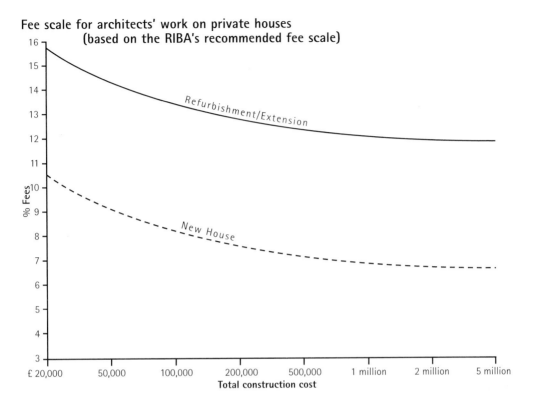

Fee scale for architects' work on private houses (based on the RIBA's recommended fee scale)

and project and for them to produce fee proposals. While this method of selecting an architect is a sign of the times, remember that it is far more important to follow your instincts and make sure that you are in sympathy with the person you appoint, even though that architect might not have submitted the lowest tender.

A la carte
There are three commonly used fee arrangements:

Percentage The fee is a percentage of the total construction cost (see p.24) of the building work. Clients are often suspicious of this since they cannot help feeling that it is in the architect's interests to increase costs and get more fees, or they ask why the architect should get more for specifying expensive items rather than cheaper ones. On the first point it is essential to establish your budget limit at the outset and impress upon your architect the necessity of keeping to it. On the second, it is true that it should be no more work to an architect to specify or draw a gold-plated tap than a chrome one, although the installation of expensive items does occasionally require extra care and coordination. It is important, however, to keep in mind that the percentage fee system is based on the principle of "swings and roundabouts": your architect might profit over the gold taps, but will spend lots of time working out the technicalities of a very cheap fixing bracket, which the percentage basis fees will hardly cover. For all parties the percentage basis can hold a large degree of uncertainty – and lead to feelings of dissatisfaction – in certain situations.

Despite this, percentage fees are still a very common form of fee agreement, although these days the RIBA guidelines are frequently ignored, both by default and in excess, depending on how "hungry" or how prestigious the selected architect is. The lowest fees charged for residential work tend to be 10 per cent, whereas some better-known practices will only agree to take on domestic work for 15–20 per cent of the cost of the works.

It is important to note that the term "total construction cost" on which the percentage is calculated relates to the sum of all items executed under the architect's direction and control, including works or materials supplied during the course of the job under different contracts or even directly by yourself. Clients often find out too late that they do not save fees if they take the kitchen out of the main contract, or buy cut-price tiles from around the corner. As long as these items have to be coordinated as part of the building contract, the architect is entitled to the fees.

Lump sum The architect will quote a fixed fee, often broken down into the main architectural stages: sketch design, detailed design, tender package and construction. Clients tend to like this method of charging, as they know where they stand. On the other hand it is essential to agree in advance how the fees will be affected should there be numerous variations to the scope or length of the job. One possibility is to "cap" the lump sum to a certain number of hours of work or to a certain value of the job. If these are exceeded, another arrangement can be in place to cover the excess work (hourly or percentage fees).

Hourly basis Traditionally, this system of charging was confined to Extra Services (see pp.25–6) – measured surveys (see p.31), feasibility studies (see p.29), party wall agreements (see pp.47–8), furniture design and so on – and to small jobs that were so difficult to quantify that any other method would have been pure speculation. Today hourly fees are commonly charged for large sections of, or indeed entire, domestic jobs, particularly below

£100,000, as it may be difficult for an architect to recoup his or her costs on a percentage basis if the client's expectations on the design and detailing are very high. Hourly rates vary tremendously, depending on, for example, the architect's experience or fame, and the nature of the job. You can be expected to pay roughly anything between £55/hr and £95/hr for a typical residential project. Junior staff should of course be charged out at a lesser rate. Clients are justifiably nervous about this method, as it is open-ended and can lead to greatly escalating fees. However, it has the advantage – for all parties involved – that it concentrates the mind. Clients who make up their minds quickly, do a lot of their own research into materials, stick to their decisions and generally leave the architect to "get on with it" might find that they would be paying less, in the end, than on any other fee basis. Clients who need to have things redesigned several times, or who require a lot of hand-holding by the architect throughout the project, are not suited to this system. From the architect's point of view it is the fairest basis on which to charge, as all work done gets paid for.

If you agree to pay on an hourly rate basis, you should of course ask your architect to give you an idea of the number of hours anticipated for the various stages of the job. Ask also for advance notice if your work is likely to exceed the total estimated number of hours, and to be kept informed, on a regular basis, of the hours worked each month.

Mix 'n' match More and more architects these days are resorting to "mixed" fee arrangements, as the architect's involvement can be estimated more accurately for some stages of the work than for others. It is not unusual therefore to find fee proposals that contain all three of the main fee bases, such as lump sum for initial design, percentage for detailed design, and hourly for construction.

Be clear!

When agreeing fees it is advisable to employ one of the three versions of the standard RIBA contract between architect and client (SFA99/CE/99/SW99), which your architect will obtain for you to sign. Make sure the architect has clearly indicated on the appropriate form which services will be provided, and enquire as to who in the design team will carry out the ones not circled by the architect (such as cost consultancy and planning negotiations). There are several optional items (Extra Services) that are not included in the Basic

Services, such as measured surveys, model-making and interior design. Agree payments by instalments. These can be monthly, or related to the completion of each stage of work, or by agreement, to suit your convenience.

Abortive work

Most architects will charge on an hourly rate for "abortive work" – that is, for work that has been designed and agreed but that will not be executed owing to various circumstances, including the following: your change of mind at a late stage; unforeseen circumstances on site that cause redesign; major alterations required by the planners or other authorities after the applications have been submitted. The last cannot always be avoided, as you often do not know in advance what the outcome of a planning decision is going to be, and yet it might have been in your interest to try to reach final design decisions at an early stage, to avoid extra expense and wasting of time.

Out of pocket

Fees are normally quoted exclusive of VAT, expenses and disbursements. Expenses usually cover travel, the printing of drawings and documents (usually a hefty expense at peak times, such as planning applications or going out to tender), telephone calls, faxes, postage, couriers, photography, "fancy" presentation materials and so on. Some clients prefer to have expenses included in the overall fee, and some offices charge a fixed percentage for expenses. You may also need to pay for disbursements, such as a

fee for a Planning Application (fixed by the council) or for the application for Building Regulations approval (on a sliding scale relating to the value of the works), although the architect might initially send a cheque on behalf of the client. Fees may vary according to which local authority is involved.

Team fees

You should also be aware that you are likely to have to pay fees to other consultants in addition to your architect. These consultants will be appointed and paid directly by yourself, although your architect might suggest appropriate names and will be able to advise you on their fee proposals. As a general rule of thumb, unless you are simply redecorating or fitting out a new kitchen or bathroom, you will almost certainly require a structural engineer. A quantity surveyor (QS) (see pp.36, 53) may be needed to help monitor costs, particularly if your project is intricate or large-scale. If you have sophisticated technical requirements, such as solar power, you may need to appoint a specialist services engineer. Other consultants will become necessary depending on the size and particular complexities of your specific job (see pp.114–15).

OH, AND YOU'LL NEED A CONSULTANT TO ADVISE ON THE CONSULTANTS !

The design stage

Defining your brief
The design period
Administrative hurdles

Defining your brief

Brief encounter

Architects, like lawyers, base their work on briefs. Architectural briefs can vary from a simple list of rooms and room areas to a complex statement of long-term intent and strategy. The basis of your brief to your architect will be your assessment of needs (see pp.9–13) and the transformation of this into a written statement of requirements. However, this will not be set in stone until completion of the feasibility studies (which investigate a variety of spatial options), as it may alter and be modified by feedback during the initial design process. If you do not have very definite ideas about what you want, your architect will help you to formulate the brief, pointing out what is possible in terms of cost and design, asking you questions and making suggestions. Your architect is also the best-placed person to help you identify the best – and worst – spatial characteristics of your property and to offer ideas that will enhance their qualities or lessen their drawbacks.

As the project progresses, it helps to keep a running checklist of items that come to mind, to be communicated at the next meeting. Try to avoid telephoning your architect every time you have a new thought, as this could interrupt the flow of the design process and affect the fees.

You can contribute at this stage by looking at books and magazines and compiling a folder with images that you especially like. However, do not expect your house to become an exact replica of a particular image that you find attractive. Literal translations are rarely possible or indeed desirable.

Intimate details

The clear communication of your thoughts and requirements to your architect is of prime importance, as it is from these that the brief, and hence the design, stems. First analyse with your architect your site or existing house and establish basic do's and don'ts. Describe your current lifestyle and how it might change, and any recurring events to allow

for, such as yearly family gatherings or visitors who stay for periods. When defining your requirements you will need to be precise about some issues – how you cook, where the washing is done, how many books and CDs you have, where you like to watch television, whether you want en suite bathrooms, whether you prefer baths or showers, and so on – and more general about others, such as the type of space or feeling you are after for particular rooms, or the relationship to the garden. Outline your stylistic preferences, including your taste in materials and buildings you have seen and liked (or disliked).

Essentials

During the course of the first meeting discuss your budget and timetable. This will enable your architect to draw up a programme, so be straightforward and direct about your resources, otherwise time will be wasted.

Hand over to your architect at the beginning all surveys and legal documents in your possession. Mention any easements over your land (for instance, a neighbour's right to cross your land to reach his or her property) and other constraints you are aware of, as these may all affect the design and what is possible. Needless to say, everything should be confirmed in writing by you or your architect.

To boldly go ...

The brief is the basis for the design and is formulated from ideas coming from you, but try not to be too conditioned by how you have lived in the past. Be open to any new ideas and suggestions that your architect may proffer.

Give all proposals and solutions serious consideration without letting habit or fixed notions unduly influence you.

Be realistic, but inspire your architect at the same time. You might be pleasantly amazed by what is possible.

The design period

Getting started

Once your brief has been defined in general terms, your architect will need to obtain an accurate measured survey of your house or site. Some architects produce their own and will charge extra fees for it, others do not and will suggest names of alternative surveyors. From this essential base drawing all the physical aspects that might affect the design can be analysed, such as orientation, vehicular access, overlooking, and direction of prevailing winds, as well as any potential conservation implications. It is important that the basic survey should be extremely accurate and show a sufficient level of detail for the job (for example, ceiling heights, window-sill heights, position of manholes, changes of materials). Photographs are an essential aid here.

Depending on the work in hand, it may be particularly important to record the type and height of any trees near the house, as this may affect the foundations of proposed extensions. Some trees, such as conifers and poplars, have extensive roots which undermine footings. There are tables that show the depth of foundations required in proximity to certain heights and species of tree, and Building Control will insist these be complied with (see p.32). This might be expensive and should be taken into account as early as possible.

Creative energy

After much talk and many negotiations, the long-awaited first drawings finally start to appear, to be followed in time by many others. This is a period of highs and lows for clients. It is easy to become extremely enthusiastic or terribly disappointed, or even to be racked by such indecision as to start doubting your own judgment. Try to control your emotions: do not fall in love with the first idea shown; likewise, do not be horrified if your architect does not hit the target the first time. For all involved, the design period is a long one, requiring many levels of refinement in concept and in detail. Rushing this period is a mistake; for the best results, creative developments should be allowed to mature naturally.

Site analysis

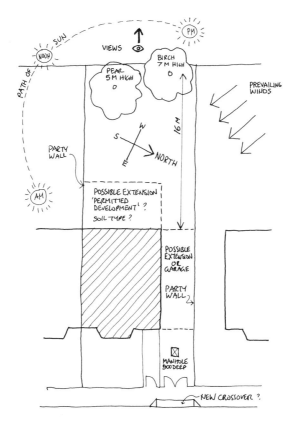

Required distance of trees from foundations

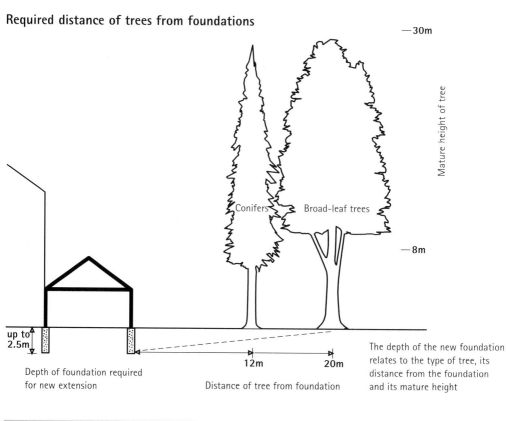

—30m

Mature height of tree

Conifers   Broad-leaf trees

—8m

up to 2.5m

Depth of foundation required for new extension

12m   20m

Distance of tree from foundation

The depth of the new foundation relates to the type of tree, its distance from the foundation and its mature height

Sketch designs

All the information having been gathered, initial sketch drawings
and draft proposals can be drawn up for your consideration. Your
architect may submit alternative, even conflicting, ideas for you to
choose between. This will help you clarify and express your own
preferences. With the help of your architect think things through.
Do not shrink from airing criticisms; it is part of the process.

Family planning ...

You may have an extended
household with children,
parents or lodgers, who might
all have differing tastes and
ideas. Everyone should be
consulted and not made to feel
left out. Your architect can
advise on the best distribution
of rooms to facilitate
circulation, avoid noise
problems and provide privacy
where needed. By talking to
each occupant, your architect should arrive at a framework that
will be functional and yet allow each participant to personalize his
or her space according to taste.

    If your family contains elderly or less able-bodied members
your architect should be able to design with them in mind, avoiding
unnecessary steps or changes of
level, specifying taps and switches
suitable for unsteady hands,
including bathrooms with non-
slip floors and suitable for wheel-
chairs, and organizing safe
kitchens with reachable controls
and storage. If you intend to stay
in your house for the rest of your
life you might consider making
provision for this now. Such
environments can be an advantage
for everyone, young and old.

Haven't got the energy

There is much talk today about environmental issues such
as sustainability, global warming and damage to the ozone layer.
Over half of Britain's total energy consumption is attributed to
buildings, whether in the form of components manufacture or
building services (heating, lighting, ventilation). While Building

Regulations take some account of this, you may like to make your own contribution towards saving the planet for your grandchildren, for example by avoiding certain materials, such as PVC and non-renewable hardwoods. You may also like to consider elements such as condensing gas boilers (in which no heat is wasted), extra-thick roof insulation, triple glazing, high-quality draught-proofing or a south-facing conservatory. As with organic foods, such items tend to cost more; but you will save on heating bills in the long run. Those mentioned are simple energy-conscious provisions; more sophisticated aspects, such as solar panels, may require a services consultant.

If you don't ask ...

Make sure that you ask lots of questions and that you fully understand what is being proposed. Do not be afraid to say that you have difficulty in "reading" plans, sections and elevations (see pp.116–17). Ask for explanations, perspective sketches or even simple models of card or polystyrene (although complex or realistic models would cost extra) to help you understand the proposals. It is imperative that you are as aware as you can be of the suggestions that are being made for your home.

The design takes shape

At the next meetings the design drawings will be much more detailed and should incorporate all the comments and requests you have made previously, plus any new ideas that these have generated in the architect's mind. Drawings will start to be at a larger scale, making it easier to imagine the space proposed. As the "design development" stage proceeds, a great deal of the architect's time will be spent ironing out inconsistencies, sorting out technical issues (drainage, structure and so on), overcoming unforeseen problems (such as difficult soil conditions) that might have arisen during preliminary investigations, and generally refining

Simple energy-saving design

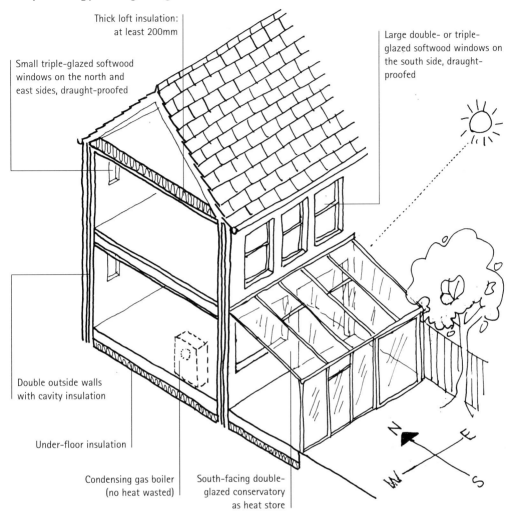

Thick loft insulation: at least 200mm

Large double- or triple-glazed softwood windows on the south side, draught-proofed

Small triple-glazed softwood windows on the north and east sides, draught-proofed

Double outside walls with cavity insulation

Under-floor insulation

Condensing gas boiler (no heat wasted)

South-facing double-glazed conservatory as heat store

the design. It is a very time-consuming period for the architect, but this is often not appreciated by the client, who cannot "see" much progress. The project is rapidly being transformed into a building, and nothing should be missed out.

Get real

Ask your architect to check costs and make sure that what is proposed is feasible within your overall budget limits. Be careful that you do not get carried away with wanting the best if you cannot afford it – remember that even small amounts add up very quickly. If your budget is limited, spend a lot of time discussing with your architect how best to spend your money and the potential ways in which you can make the most of less expensive options. "Cheap and cheerful" can be stylish or glamorous – with some thought. Good design and beautiful detailing are by no means limited to high budgets – on the contrary, the world is full of vulgar examples where money more than taste has determined the design. Your architect should also assess at this stage whether the proposed scheme complies with planning requirements, Building Regulations and conservation demands. In some instances you may feel that you have a good argument for achieving a relaxation of current regulations, possibly based on precedent or on other very individual circumstances. If this is the case, you must discuss how you intend to proceed in trying to negotiate approvals and what your fall-back strategy will be if you cannot persuade the authorities to relax their rules.

Your team

The most common consultants are a structural engineer, to provide calculations and design items such as foundations, beams, underpinning, roofs and other structural components (these need then to be submitted to Building Control for approval); and a quantity surveyor, typically for jobs over £100,000, to prepare a cost plan and tender documents, possibly Bills of Quantities, valuations of work completed by the builders and the final account. Additional consultants may include a services engineer for plumbing, heating, ventilation or electrical installations that are more complex than the standard domestic provision; a planning consultant, if you run into unusually intricate negotiations with

the council; a party wall surveyor (see p.47), if you are carrying out work to a party wall or within a certain distance from an adjoining property; an interior designer, if you require help with soft furnishings and so on; and possibly – though unlikely – a planning supervisor, to monitor various health and safely aspects during the design and construction process (the full Construction Design and Management [CDM] Regulations [1994] do not currently apply to domestic projects undertaken for a resident householder).

If there are consultants other than your architect on board, they should be brought in as early as possible in order to allow them to contribute and develop their ideas before the overall design is too advanced. Your architect will send sketch plans for the consultants' comments and design input and will organize site visits if required. For example, if you decide to remove a wall between two rooms, your structural engineer will probably want to check the structure before calculating the size of the new supporting beams required. If you have a quantity surveyor, he or she will make preliminary cost checks before preparing a budget "cost plan".

Be decisive!

Take your time in approving the design drawings, as they are the key to what follows. If you end up changing your mind later on, when the detailed technical drawings are already under way, your architect might charge you extra – for "abortive work" (see p.26) – if these have to be altered. If you need to obtain planning permission, the advanced design drawings that you have approved will be used by your architect to form the basis for the planning application. Delay and extra expense will be incurred if you ask for alterations after the submission of the application, since a new set of drawings might then have to be submitted as part of a new application.

Don't keep a dog and bark yourself

It is never too early to start thinking about materials, colours and finishes. Ask your architect for catalogues, samples and price comparisons between different items. Look through magazines and books to establish and communicate the kind of architecture and interiors you prefer. You may have decided that you want to coordinate the interior design yourself: nevertheless, it is important that you liaise with your architect in order to achieve a "look" that is integrated. Have confidence in your architect (who is trained in all design matters and should know about colour relationships) once you have made your taste known, and let him or her suggest interior schemes for discussion and approval, if this has been included in the architect's service.

Brush up your Feng Shui

Once the basic design has been agreed in principle your architect
will produce layouts showing the position of most items,
including furniture, radiators, built-in cupboards, worktops,
lighting points, power sockets, television aerial points, telephone
positions, security alarm buttons, smoke detectors and so on.
Agree the best positions for beds – facing windows or parallel to
them (to get the morning sun, if possible). Discuss the best place
for the dining table (and how it is to be lit) and other major items
of furniture.

The shopping list

At this point the tender stage draws near. You will need to discuss
in more detail and agree all the myriad items that comprise
architectural design: brick or stone colours and textures, window
types and how they open, energy-saving glass, doors (solid or
glazed), handles and locks, bathroom and kitchen fittings and
taps, built-in cupboards, wall tiles, light fittings, security fittings,
floor finishes and colours, outside paving and so on. The number
of choices to be made in a relatively short period of time is
confusing and exhausting, but ultimately very satisfying.

Cost is a prime consideration when making a decision.
Think also, however, about durability and about how each
material or element is to be cleaned and maintained. If you
have a services consultant you may want advice on more
sophisticated heating and hot-water systems.

If you have chosen any type of natural material for your
house, such as stone, marble, slate or hardwood, be prepared
for it to look different from what you expected when you saw

small samples in the shop. This is in the nature of such materials, as they come with many imperfections and variations in colour and grain. Samples tend to show the "unblemished" parts. If you want this quality all over you will need to specify that only unblemished material be used (and be prepared for this to be extremely expensive, as there will be much wastage), or be willing to select the material yourself from the supplier.

If you want to see a large range of samples before you make a decision, ensure that this is done in good time and not sprung on the architect and builders at the last minute, or you may find that delays are caused if items you want are on long delivery.

Paper is cheaper than stone

The design process is the most critical part of the whole exercise. It is essential to get the planning and design as right and as worked out as possible before progressing to the next stages. It cannot be stressed too strongly that changes of mind or trying to incorporate things left out or not thought about at the early stage will be expensive and disruptive later on, especially during the building contract. The builders will be entitled to claim extra money for being hindered in their progress, and your project could start showing evidence of piecemeal decisions. It is not worth rushing your architect (or yourself, for that matter) by trying to adhere to too tight a programme. Design is the key!

Administrative hurdles

Planning: the minefield

The most important hurdle to be cleared when proposing changes to a building, or building anew, is planning consent. Planning legislation is a minefield, and the approach to the interpretation of the Acts can differ between local authorities. Basically, planning consent in the domestic arena of architecture relates to changes in appearance or use, such as extensions or the conversion of a family house into flats and vice versa.

The granting of planning permission is part of the local democratic process. If the "development" proposed is anything but the tiniest operation, the decision on whether to allow it or not rests with the local planning committee of elected councillors. Planning officers within the planning department of the local authority are familiar with current rules and regulations, and recommend decisions to the committee. Ultimately, however, it is almost always the committee's decision that counts, and nobody can guarantee that the permission will be granted. If the application relates to an insignificant and uncontroversial issue, it might be decided "under delegated powers" by the planning officers themselves. Normally all sizes of Planning Application take a minimum of eight weeks to be resolved, largely owing to administrative hold-ups, but also because the council is obliged to post notices to all your neighbours to consult them regarding the application itself.

Submission

Almost before pen is put to paper there should be informal discussions between your architect and your local planning officer, to find out whether there are any immediate obstacles to your proposals. It is no good plunging into grand schemes only to find that there is some planning reason that precludes them.

In particular, it is very common for clients to approach architects demanding that they should obtain planning permission for schemes that are similar in scale to other ones in their street (loft extensions, rear extensions, dormer windows and so on). However, planning legislation has become significantly more stringent in recent years, and "precedent" does not necessarily buy any favours with the planners. Most cases get judged on

Planning Application form and decision notice for a kitchen/dining room extension

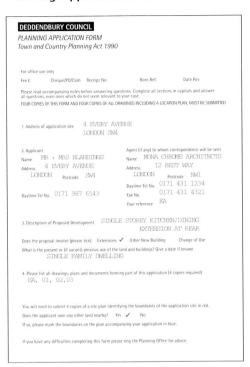

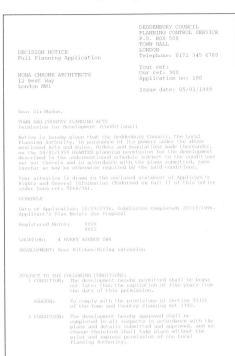

Planning Application drawing for a new-build house: front elevation

their own merits in the light of overall current planning policies, so it always helps to have your architect research the proposal thoroughly before submitting it for consideration by the planning officers. If the planners' arguments do not seem convincing, it might be worth your speaking to a planning consultant who specializes in this area and should have some useful hints and contacts; a different approach to the argument could just give you the result you are looking for and therefore justify the extra expenditure in fees.

Once your architect has prepared the planning drawings and completed the forms that constitute the submission, it is advisable to sit back and await a formal response before carrying out more work. Occasionally you will be informed early on that your case will be recommended for approval and that you stand a very good chance of being granted it; you are nonetheless at risk if you ask your architect to proceed with detailed design and technical drawings, as unforeseen objections do sometimes arise. You need written confirmation of approval before it is indisputably safe to continue.

If you do proceed with detailed design before planning consent is granted, you might find yourself incurring additional professional fees for abortive work, should substantial changes have to be made at a later date. Remember, ultimately you cannot hold your architect responsible for the outcome of the democratic planning process!

Listed buildings

Buildings in the UK of exceptional architectural interest are officially "listed" according to their status and importance. A good number of residential buildings are Listed Grade II, which means that all alterations – both to their interiors and to their exteriors – have to be approved either by English Heritage or, in areas where the local authority has taken on this role, by the council's conservation officer.

English Heritage's policies regarding listed buildings have become much more strict over the years, with a strong tendency towards preserving archaeological purity. There is concern about maintaining not only original detail (windows, doors, cornices, fireplaces, shutters, architraves) but also the original fabric of the building (lath-and-plaster ceilings and walls). These days the authorities might also insist on retaining intact the original shapes of rooms, often fighting applications to alter in any way the original plan form (such as subdividing large rooms to insert new bathrooms and kitchens). Generally, obtaining Listed Building Consent (LBC) can be even more difficult and unpredictable than getting planning permission, and you must be prepared to compromise in order to alter your listed house. If you incur great difficulties in resolving your application you might resort to speaking to historic buildings consultants, who specialize

Permitted development

What you may be able to do without planning permission if your home is not listed or in a Conservation Area. (Always check with your local council.)

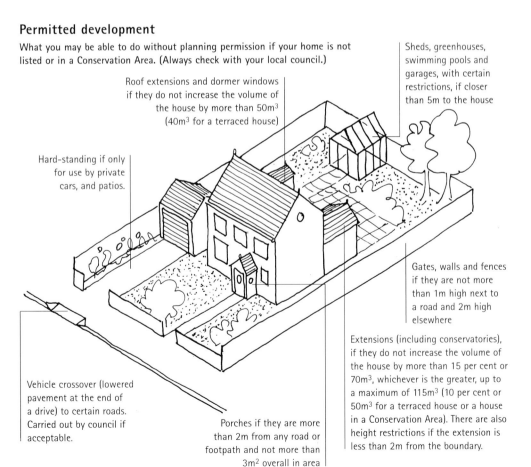

Roof extensions and dormer windows if they do not increase the volume of the house by more than 50m^3 (40m^3 for a terraced house)

Sheds, greenhouses, swimming pools and garages, with certain restrictions, if closer than 5m to the house

Hard-standing if only for use by private cars, and patios.

Gates, walls and fences if they are not more than 1m high next to a road and 2m high elsewhere

Extensions (including conservatories), if they do not increase the volume of the house by more than 15 per cent or 70m^3, whichever is the greater, up to a maximum of 115m^3 (10 per cent or 50m^3 for a terraced house or a house in a Conservation Area). There are also height restrictions if the extension is less than 2m from the boundary.

Vehicle crossover (lowered pavement at the end of a drive) to certain roads. Carried out by council if acceptable.

Porches if they are more than 2m from any road or footpath and not more than 3m^2 overall in area in mediating with English Heritage. The official duration of the process is approximately eight weeks, as with a Planning Application – although, unlike the latter, no fee is paid with the submission.

The one advantage in owning a listed building is that you will be VAT-exempt for the portion of the works that requires Listed Building Consent, as the government seeks to encourage people to look after our most precious buildings. HM Customs and Excise publishes a booklet that explains the ins and outs of taxation on listed buildings. Discuss this with your architect and builders at the beginning of your contract. Ultimately, though, the builders will sort out matters with their VAT office.

Even if your house is not listed, it might fall within a Conservation Area. In this case the planners will only be scrutinizing alterations that might affect the exterior of the building, such as height increases, changes to windows, and extensions. All these policy points need to be ascertained before your architect starts designing, if you do not wish to be disappointed later. It is advisable to approach the council from the word go, as some issue very useful booklets with design guidelines outlining do's and don'ts.

Refusal

If planning permission or Listed Building Consent is refused, and you feel it is unfair and that you have a good case, you may appeal to the Secretary of State for the Environment through your regional office. Your architect will advise on whether it is necessary to speak to a planning consultant or a specialist in historic buildings, who will assess your chances and advise you as to the best way to proceed. You must keep in mind that appealing is time-consuming (it could take six months or more), can be expensive, and is not to be undertaken lightly.

Sidestepping

If you are intending to enlarge your house by only a small amount, you might fall within what is called "permitted development" (see p.43). This generally applies to houses that are not listed, do not fall within a Conservation Area and have not been extended before. The amount you are allowed to extend before having to apply for planning permission is a fixed percentage of the volume of the existing property or 70 cubic metres for a detached or semi-detached house and 50 cubic metres for a

HE CLAIMS IT DOESNT NEED PERMISSION BECAUSE IT'S NOT A BUILDING !

terraced house, whichever is the greater. This unfortunately is often not sufficient for the use intended, except for smaller properties. Any proposed extension would also have to meet certain other criteria (height, for example) in order to be considered permitted development.

Building Control

Once planning permission has been granted, your architect will proceed to the next stage in the process: the preparation of detailed design and technical drawings. These will show all the elements of the building in much greater detail and at a larger scale. They will ultimately be used to invite tenders (see pp.50–53) from builders, and they will also be required when making an application to the council for consent under the Building Regulations.

Unlike planning permission, Building Regulations permission does not involve a committee and should not, in principle, delay your programme. So long as the detailed drawings and calculations comply with the regulations for structure, drainage, plumbing, ventilation, materials, insulation, means of escape in case of fire and so on, permission must be granted. Your architect might have to negotiate with the Building Control Officer (BCO) over how to resolve some minor issues; less frequently, you might run into a more serious impasse, often to do with regulations regarding means of escape in case of fire, which can be quite limiting in a residential context. If required, there are also specialists in this field who can guide you to alternative solutions and negotiate directly with the BCO.

In domestic projects you can choose one of two routes to obtain Building Regulations approval: submit drawings and structural calculations before you start on site (full plans application), or gain the council's approval as you go along. In the latter case the contractor submits a building notice when starting on site, and then liaises with the BCO, who inspects and approves the works at regular intervals. The advantage of the former case is that once you are on site there is no uncertainty as to the opinion of the BCO, whereas the building notice route might oblige the builders to change their method of working or detailing during the course of the works if the BCO does not approve of

Building Regulations full plans final approval

DEDDENDBURY COUNCIL

COMPLETION CERTIFICATE
Building Act 1984
Building Regulations 1991

DEDDENBURY COUNCIL
BUIDING CONTROL SERVICES

Postal address: Town Hall, PO Box 500

Office: Bevin House, SW 4

Fax: 0171 1234567
24hr answerphone: 0171 7654321
E-mail: bcontrol@dedbury.uk

MONA CHROME ARCHITECTS
12 BEST WAY
LONDON NW1

Date: 20 July 1999

Address: 4 EVERY AVENUE
LONDON SW4

Full Plans Registration No: 99/0220

Our ref: 99/0101

Case Officer: A. Gulley

Description: SINGLE STOREY REAR EXTENSION

Plot Number: 1

I confirm that, as far as could be ascertained from periodical surveys, the works referred to in the above full plans application were carried out in accordance with the requirements of the Building Regulations, as far as such work came under the jurisdiction of this Department.

Yours faithfully .... **N. Force** .... *Building Control - Development Services Division*

something, which in turn might generate unforeseen costs. Generally, and particularly for more complex and larger projects, it is best to aim for full plans applications, even though they take time to prepare and have to be fitted into an already very busy period for the architect. However, smaller projects, deemed by the architect to be uncontroversial, can be run under a building notice. Generally, Building Regulations approval is not necessary if the works comprise only minor decorative changes, such as installing a kitchen – you should check this with your architect. In terms of fees to the council, there is no difference between the two methods described above, although for the full plans approach you pay in two stages.

Once your building works are completed the BCO will "sign them off", thus giving you final approval and confirming that the works have been inspected while being carried out on site. This is an important document, which you will need if you intend to sell your house in the future.

Party walls

If you are intending to carry out work that will affect a party structure (such as a wall, fence or floor), or to build directly on your boundary line or within a specified distance of a neighbour's building, you are required by the Party Wall Act 1996 to notify all adjoining owners as to your proposed work and to make sure that you respect their rights.

Serving of notices is a complicated procedure, which can be time-consuming and expensive. Your architect may be prepared to act as a party wall surveyor (this will require a separate appointment). If not, he or she may be able to suggest a surveyor or another architect to act for you, someone who will be familiar with all the legal steps required and capable of progressing matters at a reasonable pace.

The first task to be carried out is the service of notice on the adjoining owners of the nature and extent of the works to be carried out. This must occur at least one or two months (depending on the scope of what is proposed) before the commencement of the work on site, as this period allows an adjoining owner to dissent from the works. The adjoining owners can either rely on your surveyor to monitor their interests, or appoint their own party wall surveyor to represent them, in which case you will be liable for the latter's fees. If your property abuts one in multiple ownership, you will unfortunately be obliged to serve notice on every leaseholder in the building affected by your works and on the freeholder as well, with an inevitable escalation of professional fees.

Should your surveyor and the adjoining owners' one not reach an agreement, a third surveyor must be chosen. The aim of the exercise is to arrive at a Party Wall Award, which is a

binding document that sets out in detail all matters relating to the carrying out of the proposed works, including construction methods, timing and apportioning of costs.

It is very important to ensure that your surveyor carries out a detailed inspection of the condition of the adjoining owners' property, to be included in the Award, as this will avoid any later spurious claims for damages that were not properly caused by the works.

Given the intricacies and the expense of party wall negotiations, it is sensible to consider designs that might obviate the need for a Party Wall Award. If it is unavoidable, do not take these matters lightly or postpone them, as they could have serious implications for your works.

Party wall restrictions: application of 3m and 6m rule

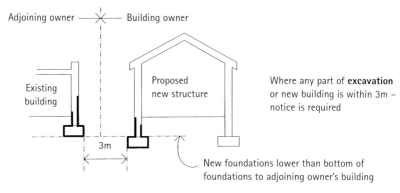

Adjoining owner ——✕—— Building owner

Existing building

Proposed new structure

3m

Where any part of **excavation** or new building is within 3m – notice is required

New foundations lower than bottom of foundations to adjoining owner's building

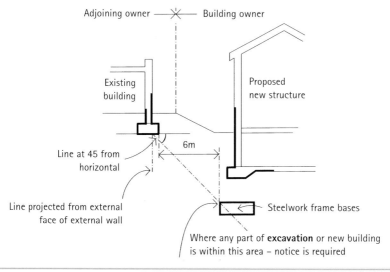

Adjoining owner ——✕—— Building owner

Existing building

Proposed new structure

Line at 45 from horizontal

6m

Line projected from external face of external wall

Steelwork frame bases

Where any part of **excavation** or new building is within this area – notice is required

The tender stage

The tender package
Selecting the contractor
The contract

The tender package

Tender care

At the end of the detailed design/technical drawings stage the information will be sufficiently complete to enable the job to be sent out to builders for competitive tendering. This is a vital stage, and it is important that you do not have changes of mind or additional requirements that will disrupt the work of your architect and team of consultants. All your professionals are working together towards completing the tender package, and even a minor change might affect a large number of related drawings and calculations. Typically, tenders are returned within three to four weeks for an average-size job.

The idea of competitive tendering is that each contractor costs the same information; consequently the tenders can be compared and analysed and the best price for the works found. The best might not necessarily be the lowest price, since if a tender is very low there may be something amiss: the builders might have left out items, or the quality of their work, while acceptable, might be noticeably inferior to the next lowest tenderer. Your architect or your QS will use his or her experience to examine the tenders and report back to you.

Alternatively, you might decide not to go out to tender; instead you can opt to negotiate a price with one or two contractors. For a job costing over £100,000 you will probably need the assistance of a QS, who will cost it independently prior to the negotiations. This method might be slightly less competitive than a full tender, but has the advantage of saving a week or two.

Tender heart

Your architect should describe the tender package to you in detail and possibly show you one similar in scope prior to producing the documents for your project. Tender packages can be more or less detailed, depending on the complexity and scale of the job, the type of builders you are approaching and whether you have a QS on board or not. It is important to assess all of the above factors before launching into your tender package; small builders will be frightened off by a very hefty and technical tender, but cynical contractors might eventually "take you to the cleaners" if you present them with a document that fails to describe in detail several items. In both cases you will end up spending more for your works, so it is worthwhile thinking your strategy through thoroughly before starting. Whichever method your architect decides to use, the aim is to describe and specify each item in as much detail as possible, so as to minimize extras during the contract when the builders chosen will no longer be in competition and might try to inflate the costs of variations.

The basic ingredients of a tender package

Working drawings These are a complete set of detailed scale drawings showing the room layouts, internal and external elevations, services, engineering drawings, joinery drawings and sufficient constructional details for the builders to price accurately the work involved.

Specification This is a vitally important document that lays down all the conditions and the quality of the contents of the building contract. It is usually in three parts, as follows:

1. Preliminaries This is priced as an independent item by the builders and includes their administrative costs, plant hire, scaffolding, insurance, foreman details and so on. It will also include details of the standard form of contract to be applied and key items such as the amount of Liquidated and Ascertained Damages (see p.59), which represents a realistic estimate of how much you would be out of pocket if the builders did not complete on time owing to reasons within their control. Any restrictions to be imposed must also be listed (see p.57), such as access or working hours, as well as commencement and completion dates, insurance and safety requirements and details of payment rates to be applied.

A contingency sum (see p.65) may also be specified. This is a nest egg to be kept for unforeseen events occurring during the work which could not be detected until exposed (dry rot, structural problems, collapsed drains, damp and so on) and is normally equal to around 10 per cent of the contract sum, depending on the condition and size of the building in question. Some architects suggest to their clients that this sum is set aside by them but not written into the contract, so as not to encourage the impression that there are "spare" funds available.

I DON'T THINK WE ALLOWED FOR THAT IN THE TENDER!

2. Materials and workmanship This covers the quality of components and finishes to be included in the building and is generally covered by standard clauses which refer to the relevant British Standard or Codes of Practice. It will also include specifications for any specialist materials or work.

3. Schedules This part lists all the contents relating to your particular job and will be set out in one of two ways, depending on the size and complexity of the works:

Schedule of Works This is an itemized list of the work to be undertaken. On smaller projects a Schedule of Works should suffice, and it is up to the tenderer to work out the precise quantities involved by reference to the detailed drawings. The schedule is usually broken down room by room, item by item, or alternatively trade by trade. This form of document suits builders who are used to "getting on with it" without too much involvement from the architect and who are known to your architect for not being very claims conscious.

Bills of Quantities The Bills of Quantities is a much more detailed "shopping list" of everything that goes into the building work. It is normally prepared by a quantity surveyor in consultation with the architect, and is thus relatively costly and usually employed on larger jobs of, say, over £200,000. The Bills of Quantities sets out the precise measurements of all the contents of the job (so many square metres of plastering, so many metre runs of skirting and so on), and each tenderer prices accordingly. This is the most accurate method of pricing and comparing tenders, and it also provides precise information on which to base any future cost variation calculations and with which to control finances.

To QS or not to QS

For small jobs your architect may deal with sending out
invitations to tender and monitoring costs, if this is included in
the agreed schedule of services contained in the architect/client
memorandum of agreement. For medium- to large-sized jobs it
is a good idea to appoint a quantity surveyor, who will prepare a
cost plan early in the design process, send out tenders and check
them for errors and discrepancies, and follow the progress on site
up to the final account. A QS is invaluable at the time of final
reckoning, that is, at the final account, as he or she will be able to
negotiate the cost of any extras to or omissions from the contract
with your builders. Although your architect can also help you in
these areas, it is a specialist field, and your outlay in QS fees could
well be recovered in the savings that may be obtained.

Selecting the contractor

Horses for courses

Before going out to competitive tender you should discuss with
your architect the number and type of builders to be invited to
submit prices. You do not want too many, but a minimum of
three or four, for a job up to £100,000, will give you a good
range of comparison. The larger the job, the more tenderers your
architect will approach, although six is a reasonable maximum
number, as tendering is expensive for the contractors and they
will become discouraged if they sense that their chances of
securing the job are slim.

Also, it is best not to include on the list any builders who
are totally "unknown" – for example, a firm that might have
written to you as part of a mail shot. In the first instance your
architect should obviously suggest contractors he or she has
worked with before and who have performed well on previous
jobs of a similar kind, explaining to you in detail their strong
points and their weaknesses. If none is available, suggestions of
names can be sought from other architects.

If you know of a good firm of builders, or someone you
trust has recommended one, discuss this with your architect.
However strong the recommendation, your architect should
always personally ask for verbal references from other architects
and clients the builders have done work for, as well as visit sites
and completed work to assess the quality of their performance. It
is not a good idea to use builders who are not used to working to
architects' designs or standard forms of contract, however low the

price. Get your architect also to enquire regarding the contractors' record on being available to offer a post-contract follow-up service. It is very useful to have continuity should you require further work in the future, as the original contractors know the house better than anyone else.

Lowest of the low?

Once tenders are in and checked, you will probably find that a few lower prices stand out. If there is one that is much lower than the others, beware. Maybe the builders have missed something vital or not understood the drawings, or think they can claim for extras at inflated prices during the course of the contract. Or maybe they are simply desperate for work, also not a good sign. Such a tender must be gone over with a fine-tooth comb by your architect or QS. Remember, you are not obliged to accept the lowest tender.

However, it is incredibly useful to analyse in detail two or three of the lowest tenderers. While it is not in your interest to "squeeze" your contractors from day one, try to negotiate and ask them whether they are able to make any suggestions for reducing the overall costs. Remember also that you will get what you pay for. If you select a cheaper contractor, you cannot expect a Rolls-Royce performance.

You should find out which subcontractors the builders intend to use, whether they have their own joinery-making facilities, who the site foreman will be and so on. You cannot be too careful at this stage: being landed with incompetent builders is the worst kind of nightmare.

Mr (or Ms) Right

In the end, however, you must feel happy with the people who are going to rip your lovely house apart and put it back together over the next months. Follow your instincts and if you have any feelings of doubt regarding the builders' representative, no matter how many checks have

been done on them, think twice. Maybe you don't like the way they present themselves, or perhaps they are too familiar. Of course, all builders will be bending over backwards to please and show they are efficient before they have landed the job (what some architects call the "honeymoon period"); this is only natural. But once work starts and problems arise, attitudes can change; again, this is par for the course. So be quite sure you are happy with the builders and foreman and can establish a relationship with them based on trust rather than enmity.

Money matters

Whoever the builders chosen, your architect needs to check their insurance levels and do a financial check on the company and its credit facilities. The builders may also request bank references from you and ask how the project will be funded. Small builders always worry about delays in payment as they require an even cash-flow to finance the work. Never agree to pay money "up-front" to the contractor, and only pay for work that your architect has certified is complete and to standard. On no account agree to cash payments to avoid VAT: this is illegal, and could land you in hot water should there be disputes or if the builders go bust. Also, do not contemplate paying subcontractors directly, as you will still be obliged to pay the builders (or their receiver). Yes, it can occur that builders go into bankruptcy during a contract; you hope it will never happen, but it can. You may obtain some sort of guarantee by asking for a "performance bond" – a sum of money the builders' bank holds in case of default – but this invariably increases the cost of tenders and is only really justified in a larger project.

The contract

Pre-contract

Once you have selected your preferred contractors for the job, your architect should arrange a pre-contract meeting in order to run through the following items, which will have been set out in the tender documents, to ensure that there are no misunderstandings.

- **Length of contract**
- **Frequency of payments** This is usually four-weekly intervals but may be reduced to two- or three-weekly for a small builder on a small job. Occasionally the contractor might offer a reduction in price if payments are made more frequently.
- **Hours of working** Your neighbours will not take kindly to being woken up by drilling at 6.00am or at weekends. There will probably be local authority regulations regarding noise, nuisance and working hours.
- **Use of services** These comprise lavatory, electricity, water and telephone. Small builders may ask for free use of water but should pay for electricity. You can ask the builders to provide their own (chemical) lavatory, but you will have to pay for it. Today most builders have their own mobile phones.
- **Access, storage and site boundaries** Stipulate the way in which the materials will be brought onto the site: often difficult if it is in the middle of a terrace or on a floor above ground level. Stipulate precisely which areas are part of the site and which are off limits. If builders see a piece of ground they are likely to cover it with materials. If you do not want your exquisite garden destroyed, stipulate the positioning of a barrier beyond which is out of bounds to contractors. Similarly, if you want to leave furniture in the house, put it in a locked, sealed room. Dust and dirt get everywhere on a building site, and there is no way round this. If you live in a flat, it is strongly recommended that the contents go into storage. Think ahead of ways to prevent damage to your belongings, thereby avoiding much anger and frustration.
- **Site meetings** Your architect will stipulate the frequency and day of builders' site progress meetings and who chairs them. Typically they occur weekly or every two weeks, although the architect might inspect the site more frequently during

particular phases of the job. Do not expect your architect
to be on site daily; this is not necessary if the drawings are
complete and the builders know their business. You can ask
to be present at site meetings, but they tend to be boring and
technical and you may prefer to keep up to date on progress
by reading the minutes.

- **Administrative arrangements** Architect's Instructions (AIs),
  minutes, valuations and so on (see pp.62–3).
- **Variations (see p.63)** Discuss the arrangements for pricing for
  extras and omissions (see p.73). These always occur, and it is
  the architect's job to price them on a fair and reasonable basis.
  Nevertheless it is good to establish at the beginning that
  everybody involved (including you) is going to be reasonable
  about them, possibly setting up a system by which prices for
  major items can be agreed before work is carried out.
- **VAT** VAT on building work is constantly changing. You
  should have been informed of the current regulations by
  your architect, particularly if your house is listed. In the end,
  however, the builders will have to sort out VAT with their own
  tax office and refer back to you. Your architect will be unable
  to give you definite answers on the details.
- **Foreman** Confirm whether a full-time foreman will be
  employed on the job and what his or her trade or training is.
  The foreman is the key figure on site, and will not be
  concerned with costs but more with the standard of the work.
  For very large jobs, clients may appoint their own site agent,
  known as the clerk of works, to monitor progress and
  standards.
- **After-care** The contract will specify a Defects Liability
  Period (see pp.59, 70), but if it is a condition of the tender
  documents it is a good idea to remind the builders that they
  shall provide all necessary manuals and guarantees and identify
  the positions of pipes and wiring.

The contract

It is essential to enter into a proper
contract with your builders. The standard
form of contract employed is most often
one of those drawn up by the Joint
Contracts Tribunal (JCT) Ltd, although
there are several other kinds, and their
length, detail and complexity depend on
the size of the job. For smaller domestic
jobs there is the Minor Works Agreement
(MW98), for middle-sized schemes the
Intermediate Form of Building Contract

(IFC98), and for very large (usually not domestic) projects the Standard Form of Building Contract (JCT98). Like all such documents these contracts are couched in legal jargon and, unless you are a High Court judge, you may need your architect to interpret the clauses for you.

In principle the contract will establish:
- the name of the architect or contract administrator (CA)
- the contract sum
- the start and completion dates for the works
- the amount and proof of Public Liability Insurance carried by the contractors, and the insurance level for the works
- the frequency of interim (stage) payments (see p.63)
- the amount of Retention (see p.63), usually 5 per cent until Practical Completion (see pp.68–9) and 2.5 per cent until the end of the Defects Liability Period
- the Defects Liability Period (see p.70), usually six months, although you can ask for twelve
- the rate of Liquidated and Ascertained Damages for non-completion (see p.73). This is not a "penalty clause", as some clients think, but a sum reflecting a genuinely anticipated loss to the client per week, which may be deducted or claimed if the contract overruns owing to reasons within the control of the builders
- arrangements for arbitration in case of disputes
- clauses relating to VAT and labour rates
- clauses relating to variations to the contract
- clauses relating to determination of the contract

As stated previously, the contract documents will comprise a standard contract, the tender drawings and the specification, including the priced Schedule of Works or Bills of Quantities. Copies of the documents will need to be signed by both you and the builders. Signed contracts and documents are then exchanged. Keep your copy safe, and do not take the drawings out and use them to get prices for carpets and so on.

The construction stage

On site

Practical completion

Moving in

Final tasks

On site

A site for sore eyes

Well before the day the building contract starts, you will need to clear out all your property from the affected parts of the house. Do not expect the contractors to do this unless it has been agreed and priced as part of the contract. Belongings left exposed will almost certainly get damaged, lost or stolen, and it is not fair to impose the responsibility for them on the builders. If items have to be left put them in a locked and sealed room (see p.57).

Your architect will have identified those items to be "set aside" (wrapped and stored) for reuse. These might be doors, fireplaces, mirrors and suchlike that you want incorporated in the final design. Keep your own list of these and their condition.

Impress on all parties which areas are to be protected or are out of bounds (see p.57). Discuss site safety with your architect.

You should take care when visiting the site, and wear appropriate shoes, and a hard hat, mask or gloves if required. Skirts and kilts should be avoided if you are climbing ladders. A tetanus booster will protect you from the risk posed by rusty nails. Generally you should not visit the site unless accompanied by the architect, and it is not a good idea to bring young children on to the site; if you do, keep a tight hold on them. Your architect will advise you when it is a good time to visit the site, to see the most significant recent changes. The frequency of your visits will vary, depending on the stage of the job, from every few weeks at the beginning to every few days at the end. Avoid breathing down the contractors' necks; it does not speed them up.

MAY I INTRODUCE THE CLIENT ?

It's good to talk

Lines of communication are vital once work starts on site, but they should only be via your architect, to whom you should address all instructions or queries. Although you might find this system hard to respect if you visit the site more frequently than your architect does, it is a cardinal rule to be adhered to if he or she is to keep control of the job and the costs. Ignore it at your peril!

Regular site meetings (see p.57) bring the construction team together to monitor progress, identify action to be taken and keep everyone informed. You are not expected to attend these meetings,

Architect's Instruction

Issued by: address:	Mona Chrome Architects 12 Best Way London NW1		**Architect's instruction**
Employer: address:	Mr and Mrs Blandings 4 Every Avenue London SW4	Serial no:	07
		Job reference:	EA
Contractor: address:	J.Retch Construction Ltd 13 Cavity Close London W3	Issue date:	12.4.99
		Contract dated:	19.3.99
Works: Situated at:	Extension and Improvements 4 Every Avenue London SW4		

Under the terms of the above Contract, I/We issue the following instructions:

	Office use: Approx costs	
	£ omit	£ add
1. **Structure**. Spec Ref 28.9 Remove rotted joists and floor-boards to front of lower ground floor kitchen. Fix 50 x 100 treated softwood joists and new floorboards.		780
2. **Utilities**. Spec Ref A.54 Accept Transco's quotation dated 12th January 1999 for the sum of £151.60. **Omit**: Provisional sum £150	150	151.60
3. **Windows**. Spec Ref 36.4 **Omit**: New sash window W5 to rear elevation. **Add**. Repair, ease and reglaze existing sash. Provide draught proofing to BS 874.	390	250
4. **Drainage**. Spec Ref 14.9 **Add**: Trapped yard gulley to rear patio Make connection to man-hole 2.		135

To be signed by or for
the issuer named
above.   Signed _____

Amount of Contract Sum	£ 173,200 —
± Approximate value of previous instructions	£ 2,600
	£ 175,800
± Approximate value of this instruction	£ 1 056.60
Approximate adjusted total	£ 176,856.60

Distribution	☒ Employer	☒ Quantity Surveyor	☐ Services Engineer
	☒ Contractor	☒ Structural Engineer	☒ File
	☐ Nominated Sub-Contractors		

© 1985 RIBA Publications Ltd

but you should read the minutes carefully and raise any questions with your architect as soon as possible. The minutes are important documents and will be used as evidence if disputes arise.

Proposed variations to the contract and their potential cost implications should be brought to your attention as soon as they arise. Once they are agreed, your architect will issue an Architect's Instruction (AI), a standard form itemizing all additions and omissions, with copies to you, the builders and the QS, who will price them. If you do not have a QS on board it might be useful if the builders price the variations before executing the AI. Alternatively, it can be negotiated by your architect at the time of the final account. Minor urgent changes can be agreed by your architect on site by a written instruction to be confirmed within a set time by an AI.

Pay now, live later

At stages agreed previously and inserted in the contract, your architect or QS will check the work completed on site and produce a valuation of the cost of properly executed items, plus materials and components delivered to the site, against the prices in the Schedule of Works. The builders may submit their own valuation beforehand for the architect's consideration. Your architect will then issue an Interim Certificate to you for payment, including the deduction for Retention (see p.59), which you are obliged to pay within 14 days. Failure to do so would be a breach of contract and may disrupt small builders who depend on regular cash-flow to subsidize the work. Items of joinery or materials ordered but not delivered should not normally be included in the Interim Certificate.

Led up the critical path

Once demolition starts, you will be surprised at the speed with which things happen and possibly dismayed as you see your property reduced to dust and rubble. Owners may get alarmed and depressed and feel they have made a huge mistake. Keep faith. For your architect it is a very exciting time as the decks are cleared and the house is purged of old eyesores.

MY POOR HOME!

Certificate for interim (stage) payment

Certificate for
**Interim/
Progress
Payment**

Issued by: **Mona Chrome Architects**
address: **12 Best Way**
London   NW1

Employer: **Mr and Mrs Blandings**   Serial no: **B 157147**
address: **4 Every Avenue**
London   SW4   Job reference: **EA**

Contractor: **J.Retch Construction Ltd**   Certificate no: **2**
address: **13 Cavity Close**
London   W3   Issue date: **12.4.99**

Works: **Extension and Improvements**   Valuation date: **8.4.99**
situated at: **4 Every Avenue**
London   W4   Contract sum: **£89,000**

Contract dated: **19.3.99**   Original to Employer

This Certificate for Interim/Progress Payment is issued under the terms
of the above-mentioned Contract.

A. Value of work executed and of materials and goods on site
(excluding items included in E below) .... £ **14,471.00**

[1] Percentage is normally 95% except where Practical Completion has been achieved (97½%) or where some other percentage has been agreed by the parties

[1] B. Amount payable (**95**   % of A) .... £ **13,747.45**

[2] This item applies to IFC 84 only. Delete for MW 80 or if not relevant to this Certificate.

[2] C. Release of retained percentage on partial possession .... £

[2] D. Payment for goods and materials off site .... £

[2] E. Amount payable (or deductible) at 100%
in accordance with IFC 84 clause 4·2·2 .... £

Sub-total £ **13,747.45**

Less amounts previously certified .... £   **8,220.00**

Net amount for payment .... £   **5,527.45**

I/We hereby certify that the **amount for payment** by the Employer to the
Contractor on this Certificate is (in words)

Five thousand, five hundred and twenty seven

pounds and 45p

All amounts are exclusive of VAT

To be signed by or for the issuer named above

Signed _____

[3] Relevant only if clause A1·1 of IFC 84 Supplemental Conditions or clause B1·1 of MW 80 Supplementary Memorandum applies. Delete if not applicable

[3] The Contractor has given notice that the rate of VAT chargeable on the
supply of goods and services to which the Contract relates is **17½** %

[3]   % of the amount certified above is .... £

[3] Total of net amount and VAT amount (for information) .... £

This is not a Tax Invoice

F851 for IFC 84, MW 80   © RIBA Publications Ltd 1990

Often operations on site start out with a series of startling discoveries that could not have been foreseen, such as dry rot, cracked drains, weak foundations or the remains of a Roman villa. In most cases your contingency sum (see p.52) should be large enough to cope (there are not many Roman villas!). Again, such setbacks or extras may induce panic or regret. Be positive. Remember that your architect will have seen it all many times before and is equipped to deal with most things.

Following demolition, the normal sequence of work is:
- **Structural work** Foundations, new walls, forming openings for windows or doors, putting in new beams and joists for floors and roofs, and so on
- **Drainage** The underground drain pipework, new manholes and gullies, connection to the sewer
- **Services** Gas, water and electrical mains
- **First fix** Carpentry "carcassing", heating and plumbing pipework, electrical wiring
- **Plastering and cement floor screeds**
- **Second fix** Bathroom fittings, radiators, sinks, joinery, doors, kitchen units, light fittings, and so on
- **Finishes** Wall and floor tiling, painting, hardwood flooring, and so on
- **External works** Patio paving, car hard-standing, garden walls, landscaping, and so on

Killing time

Usually, the builders will issue at the start of the works a bar chart programme showing each stage and trade and how they overlap (see p.66). Ask your architect to explain this to you. It is not uncommon with work to old houses for the contract to overrun as there are many unpredictable disruptions to the smooth running of the job, and you may become anxious over delays and costs with no end in sight. The builders must notify the architect if the works will not be completed by the agreed date. Only if the delays are due to one of

the reasons permitted in the contract will an extension of time be granted. Furthermore, the builders may try to claim extra costs for the additional time they have to be on site with plant and labour. Whether they are entitled to these will depend on the terms of the contract and the reason for the delay. Not every reason will entitle the builders to claim. For example, an extension of time may be

Contractors' programme

Jan	Feb	Mar	Apr	May	Jun	Jul	Aug	Sep

By Main Contractors

Excavation

Concreting

Bricklaying

Carpentry

Joinery

Plumbing

Painting

Painting

By Sub-Contractors

Steel frame

Heating

Plastering

Slating

Asphalt

Electrician

Glazing

Glazing

Flooring

granted for exceptional weather conditions, but in this case you would not be required to pay the loss and expense costs, including "prelims" costs (plant on site), that the builders have put in the tender for each week the contract is extended. If the builders fail to complete on time where no extension of time has been given, your architect will advise you that under the terms of the contract you may apply the Liquidated and Ascertained Damages (see p.59) clause and deduct the agreed amount from future payments. The builders will probably dispute this and mount counter-arguments. The architect is the judge of where the responsibility for the delay lies and must be impartial when making any decision. Again, this may be worrying for the layperson, but it is a normal occurrence.

The end is nigh

During the initial stages you may be alarmed that the project is not as you envisaged, rooms appear dark and mean, wires and pipes snake about everywhere, chaos reigns. But once the "nice bits", the finishes, start going in, towards the end, your mood will probably change to one of great excitement. Do not be downhearted if some things turn out not to be straightforward here, either – perhaps the tiles delivered are not the ones ordered, the kitchen is late, or colours are not what you wanted. Despite your frustration, keep in mind that the end result will justify all your initial anxieties and you will enjoy the fruits of these endeavours for years to come.

It is often difficult to convey to clients that any changes of mind during these later stages will have a significant effect both on progress and on costs. Any proposed variations should be considered very carefully to determine whether or not they are really essential. Building is not like dressmaking, where the length of a hem can rise or fall according to whim or sleeves can be altered at will. Late changes are much more demoralizing for the builders and can often severely compromise the standard of the finished item.

At this point you will be discussing the difference (if any) between the original contract completion date and the actual one, the reasons for this and what action needs to be taken. As the light at the end of the tunnel appears, always allow some extra time before you plan to move in, but do not tell the builders about it! Avoid setting your moving-in date around a particular event such as Christmas, children's holidays or a family occasion. Also avoid organizing a huge housewarming party before you have actually moved in. There is a great deal to do when you move in, and you will not be able to tell for a while when the house or flat will be ready to welcome people in a formal manner. The coincidence of moving in with another major occasion is a nice idea in theory, but it often causes a lot of extra pressure and anxiety, or disappointment when the date cannot be met.

Discuss with your architect in advance which items you might want to install under a separate contract after Practical Completion (see pp.68–9), such as carpets, curtains or landscaping, and coordinate them in such a way as not to interfere with the final stages of the main building works.

It is now that Building Control should issue the final certificate of compliance with the Building Regulations. Remember that altering crucial safety items immediately after the last inspection, such as taking off automatic door-closers, might invalidate your household insurance as well as being dangerous for members of your family.

Practical completion

Hitting a snag

It is the builders' responsibility to build the work according to the
contract. The architect will inspect to see that this is done and will
make it clear to the contractors where the standards are not good
enough. The architect will advise the contractors of any defective
work that needs to be put right, such as missing knobs, poor
paintwork, noisy radiators and dripping taps,
and will repeat the inspection several times
as items are put right and new ones appear.
During your site visits with your architect
you could make your own snagging list of
minor defects to be rectified, but do not
take this as an opportunity to get out a
magnifying glass and search for faults.
Be guided by your architect as to what
constitutes a defect. In some cases, problems
such as a chip in your enamelled steel bath
surround cannot be rectified satisfactorily
without causing huge disruption. Discuss
this with your architect, including the
option of negotiating a financial reduction
to compensate for an unsatisfactory result.

     Practical Completion finally occurs when the main work
is finished and all visible defects up to that point have been put
right. Only very minor things should be left, unless you have
specifically agreed otherwise with the architect and builders.
These should not inconvenience you in taking possession of the
house or refurbished rooms. The exact definition of Practical
Completion can lead to disagreement with the contractors, as they
stand to gain financially by receipt of the certificate. Your architect
will determine impartially when the job has reached Practical
Completion and issue a certificate to that effect. At this point the
penultimate certificate for payment will be issued, showing that
half the 5 per cent Retention will be released, and the contractors
cease to be liable for the insurance to the property. Remember
that Practical Completion is not the real end of the contract; this
comes when your architect issues the Final Certificate (see p.73)
after the six (or more) months' Defects Liability Period (see p.70).

The finishing tape

Although it is important to keep the momentum going for
the whole team as the job nears its end, do not try to rush the
final stages unnecessarily. These are most crucial in terms of

the pleasure you will derive from your transformed home, and it would be a pity to spoil the quality of the work simply for the sake of a few days. Even more importantly, try not to have last-minute changes of mind over decorations or finishes. Having to deal with such alterations at a late stage is very difficult; to undo, move or change things has a domino effect and can put the whole programme back by affecting all following trades. Even apparently small changes can damage the overall quality of the job – so do not be tempted to move light-fitting positions, for example, after the walls have been plastered.

Miracles cost a bit more

Architects often find that clients become obsessive about the quality of workmanship both during the course of the contract and post-completion. You must rely on your architect to judge whether the work has been carried out to the standard specified in the contract, and not expect machine precision where cheaper materials have had to be employed. It must be stressed that the quality of the contractors' work is reflected in the price you have agreed to pay. If you have selected "budget" builders you cannot expect Rolls-Royce perfection. This having been said, a reasonable professional standard should always be expected, and no sloppy or poor workmanship should be accepted.

It is a question of finding a happy medium.

Moving in

And so to bedlam

Moving in is the time of your greatest expectations and greatest
frustrations. You are so near and yet so far. It is utterly maddening
and nobody seems to be able to help. You are furious with your
builders, impatient with your architect and ready to kill your
partner. Many things will go wrong: the heating will not work,
taps will come off, showers will leak. Do not
lose your cool; keep a running list for your
architect to deal with. You should be warned
that it takes roughly three months to move
into a new house properly. The first few
days are bedlam, then things improve to
mere chaos. There is a long, hard task in
front of you, plus much fine-tuning by the
builders. This is reality. Do not expect
anything less. Moving in is never smooth.

   You will find that the builders might
need to return by arrangement, even though
you cannot stand them any more. They will
be putting up the last of the shelves and
tweaking the heating system. This is the
nature of completing a project, unless you have allowed the
builders a long and generous contract period. Even then old
Murphy's Law applies, and there are always last-minute things
that need to be completed.

   The builders will give the house a "builders' clean",
which includes dusting, vacuuming, and washing windows and
bathrooms, but you will have to organize your own in-depth
cleaning. Do not do this too early, or you will find you will
have to do it twice. Dust will be settling for months and there
is nothing you can do about it.

Just teething pains

Think of this period in your home as a (clenched) teething period.
It is officially called the Defects Liability Period (see p.59), after
which the builders must return and make good any defects which
have appeared since Practical Completion (see pp.68–9), though
obviously not any caused by you. It is always good to let at least
two seasons go by before the end of the DLP so that you will have
had the heating both on and off, and any swelling or shrinkage
will have become apparent. Expect some cracks to appear in the
plaster and in joinery, particularly at the junction of different
materials, and in wall or floor tiles. For some reason, light bulbs

tend to "pop" very frequently once building work stops. This is probably because of all the knocking and vibration during the course of the work and is not necessarily a sign of poor fittings or bad workmanship.

Ask your architect to ensure your builder provides you with the guarantees and instruction booklets for all the mechanical and electrical systems. Keep them safely and follow the advice on maintenance. Get the subcontractors to instruct you on how to operate all systems safely and efficiently.

Home alone

Clients often find it difficult to "let go" of their architect. The relationship has ideally been a fruitful one and the interaction positive over many months. It is quite normal to want to sustain the sharing aspect of the experience once you move in, but as time passes you will have to stand on your own feet and rely on your own judgment about furnishing your home and living in it. If you are intending to refurbish your house substantially, buying new furniture and getting rid of possessions that you have had for years, it is advisable to take plenty of time over it. Do not rush this phase; try to get a real feel for the house before choosing things to put in it. Buy items that are appropriate for the style of architecture you will be living in. Ask shops if you can obtain furniture on approval, and consult books and magazines. This is another design phase and should not be underestimated.

When you first move in you will be obsessively searching for imperfections in the house, either flaws in workmanship, aspects of the design that irritate or things that you now feel you would have done differently. Your eyes are attuned to the small-scale details and you notice everything. After a time you will feel a bit more distant and these details will niggle less. You are living comfortably in your home and beginning to love it. However, as the weeks go by, things become less perfect still as they scratch, break, stain or crack. This always happens when you live in a house, but, although the exhilarating feeling of newness goes, a "lived-in" patina is gradually acquired and with it a satisfying feeling of belonging. Some people learn to love their new home immediately, others experience a form of mild depression for the first few months.

You will need to grow into your house, find places for things, develop new habits. It is a process of getting to know your spaces and it takes time and patience. You will learn that a house is a living thing, with its infancy and maturity, its foibles and moods. It communicates.

Final tasks

Fair and square

During the Defects Liability Period the builders should submit their final account to your architect or QS for scrutiny. The final account will include all the extras or omissions previously agreed, although there will probably be some negotiations or even "horse trading" to achieve a fair conclusion of all outstanding matters. Bear in mind that your architect is supposed to act impartially and is not there to try to prevent the builders from getting proper payment for work completed. Some clients do not understand this and feel that, as they employ the architect, the latter should use

every trick to beat the builders down; if this does not occur, they instantly think the architect is "taking the builders' side". It is the architect's professional and moral obligation to be fair and reasonable towards all parties. It is in your interest that there should be a certain amount of give and take between yourself and the contractors. Do not attempt to be too rigid or dogmatic, as this could involve you in much more expense (see below).

At the end of the six months' (or more) Defects Liability Period, your architect will advise the contractors of any final defects that may have appeared post-completion and will ensure that the builders return to put them right. Your architect will issue a Final Certificate within the time-scale set out in the contract, probably (but not necessarily) after agreement has been reached by all. At this point the balance of the Retention (2.5 per cent) shown on the architect's penultimate payment certificate (see p.68), and issued to coincide with Practical Completion, should be released to the builders.

Agreeing to differ

If the contract has overrun and your architect feels that the builders have been delayed by events that do not justify an extension of time, you will be advised that, under the terms of the contract, you can deduct the sum specified under Liquidated and Ascertained Damages (see p.59) from any future payment. This is your decision, but be guided by your architect. Should the builders not agree with your architect's decisions regarding the final account or extensions of time, they may proceed to adjudication, arbitration or litigation as allowed for in the contract.

Adjudication (among other things) was introduced into all building contracts after 1 May 1998 to comply with the Housing Grants, Construction and Regeneration Act 1996. The application of the Act is not, in fact, compulsory in construction contracts with residential occupiers, and you can discuss with your architect whether or not to include this clause in your contract. In some cases adjudication can be a good idea. Either you or the builders can refer disagreements under the contract to an independent person, who adjudicates on the matter very quickly

(usually within four weeks). His or her decision is binding, and will be enforced by a court if necessary, but either side may then decide to refer the whole matter to either arbitration or litigation, whichever the contract states.

In addition to adjudication, most standard forms of building contract allow the parties to choose whether disputes are resolved by arbitration or by litigation. This might arise where both parties feel that adjudication may not be suitable for a particular dispute (perhaps it is too complex to be satisfactorily resolved within four weeks), or where they disagree with a decision reached by an adjudicator. The choice between arbitration and litigation should be discussed with your architect before the tender documents are sent out. Frequently people prefer arbitration because it is confidential. Another advantage of arbitration (and adjudication) is that the arbitrator can be an architect (not your architect) or a surveyor, and will therefore have a good understanding of the industry. If your architect is involved in the proceedings he or she will also have to be paid on an hourly rate, as the original contract between you and your architect is now terminated. Be sure of your case before embarking on the adjudication or arbitration process or it could cost you more in the long run than being flexible over the final account. Of course, if the builders decide to refer something to adjudication or arbitration, you will have little choice but to comply. In arbitration it is usual to be represented, because procedures tend to be quite formal and legalistic. Although the winner is normally awarded costs, these may amount to only 60–85 per cent of the expenditure. Arbitration is final and binding, and the award is enforceable by a court if necessary. An appeal is possible but not usual. If you become embroiled in these processes you will need expert advice.

Disputes between architects and clients should also be mentioned. These are usually to do with fees, or are sometimes questions of competence. Once again the RIBA standard forms of appointment with your architect indicate that the dispute should be resolved by adjudication and/or arbitration. The RIBA operates a very useful conciliation service which may stop disputes getting out of hand. You may lodge a complaint with the Architects' Registration Board if you feel the matter is sufficiently serious. All registered architects must carry Professional Indemnity Insurance against claims of negligence and may be insured for recovery of fees.

Keep fit for purpose

Ask your architect for copies of all the Planning and Building Control consents; you may need them when it comes to reselling. It might be interesting to obtain a valuation from an estate agent once the work is completed – you may be pleasantly surprised by the escalation in value of your property. Architectural design, if successful, pays off. Encourage your architect to get your house or project featured in a magazine. This will be pleasing for you (and you can impress your friends) and good for potential buyers in the future.

You should organize adequate maintenance for your refurbished or new home. Over the following years things will start needing repair, redecorating and general love and care. Your builders are not necessarily the best people to use for this, as it may not be cost effective for them, but you should always consult them first on anything major related to the main contract itself.

For small jobs, find a reputable handyman, a good plumber and a reliable electrician. The regular upkeep of your house is as important as keeping yourself healthy and fit. Remember that the constantly changing climate in our island state weathers buildings quickly. Paintwork cracks and peels, wood shrinks and expands, water attempts to penetrate everywhere, damp is a constant threat, humidity is rife in hot summers, and snow and frost in winter can attack pipes and gutters. You may yearn for white stuccoed Mediterranean walls shining under the sun, but in Britain they will soon become distressed by climate and pollution. This is why the traditional British brick and tile or slate house is so successful: these materials need little regular maintenance if properly built. Needless to say, some people paint their bricks or stick mock stone over them, thus giving themselves an ongoing redecoration challenge. Expertise is expensive, but ignorance is even more so.

Architecture for all

If all has gone well, when all the stress and upset are over you will be the proud possessor of a piece of architecture of your very own, a transformed environment designed to suit your specific requirements. Architecture is not defined only as large monumental buildings but can be any piece of design, however small in scale, that communicates pleasure and enhances comfort. You may have gone for wacky post-modern, cool minimalist or sensible domestic, but the style and workability will have been determined by your particular taste and preferences, in a custom-built expression of your unique personality.

We hope that this guide has helped to demonstrate the highly complex nature of design and implementation if they are properly carried out. To achieve the feel-good factor referred to above, and guarantee a reasonably successful result, we believe there is only one safe method. Do it with an architect!

Doing it partly with an architect

If you cannot afford all the fees, then, rather than compromise the quality of your refurbishment, discuss with an architect the following possible alternatives:

- revisiting the brief
- phasing
- partial services

Revisiting the brief Your initial thoughts might be extravagant and unrealistic in relation to your budget. An architect can help you find acceptable practical solutions that will provide the spatial and aesthetic gains desired without breaking the bank. An architect's knowledge of materials can be extremely useful in achieving an elegant design solution without using top-of-the-range products. Good design does not necessarily imply expensive materials and finishes.

Phasing In discussion with your architect, you might decide that it makes more economic sense not to carry out all the work at once. While it is usually best to complete as much as possible of the structural work and essential repairs in one go, you can easily leave for a later time decorations, joinery, carpeting and suchlike. Once again, be advised as to the best phasing arrangements; your architect will know about the sequencing of trades and how to phase the job without causing extra works (and consequently extra cost).

Partial services If you employ an architect for only part of the job, you must resign yourself to the fact that the end product will probably not be as satisfactory as if you had had the luxury of the full service. Most builders and surveyors do not have the training, aesthetic judgment and eagle eye for details that a talented architect has, and try as they may to implement exactly the architect's drawings, if the architect is not following the job through on site, the end result may suffer. Remember, also, that the administration and organization associated with a building job is very intricate, and that you may get out of your depth if you take it on yourself. So you must think long and hard before deciding to retire your architect from the scene after the design stages.

- If you really cannot afford the full service, you will still obviously gain benefit from your architect's input for as long as you can afford his or her fees. You might decide to employ an architect for a brief consultation or up to submission of the

Planning Application, or to the end of design development
and tender. If you cannot afford fees for the full contract
administration on site, you might still arrange that your architect
will be in attendance and available to give you a few one-off
consultations if you run into problems. If your heart is really set
on a particular individual architect, because you especially like
his or her style, but you cannot afford the prima donna fees,
maybe you can reach an arrangement with the practice that will
allow you to use a more junior, less experienced architect or a
surveyor for the construction phases.

● Do discuss with your architect the best way forward, as
he or she will be as keen as you are to see your job properly
executed. However, avoid being penny-wise and pound-foolish:
consider omitting the gold taps before you think of replacing your
architect with a surveyor recommended by the estate agent.

Projects

"Dad, the photographer's here to take pictures of our new kitchen extension."

A garden extension

A study

A loft conversion

A kitchen extension

A three-storey extension

A flat conversion

A town-house conversion

A rural conversion

A self-build house

A new-build house

A garden extension

The client A single man in the medical profession.

The property A semi-detached double-fronted Victorian house divided into three apartments. The client owns the ground- and first-floor apartments. The house is situated in a wide tree-lined road in a North London Conservation Area. Many houses in this area have rear extensions built over the past 30 years with no distinctive style.

The brief The architect was asked to create two new apartments within the lower two floors of the house. The client intended to sell the first-floor apartment once it had been fitted out and to retain the ground-floor apartment, with its substantial garden, for his own use. The aim was to transform the ground floor into a modern home and a sanctuary that felt far away from the city.

The architect Walters and Cohen.

Administrative issues

Planning Permission and Conservation Area Consent Planning permission was obtained for the construction of a modern rear extension and a glazed conservatory despite considerable opposition from neighbours. They were against the scheme because they felt that the design should be more in keeping with that of the main house and the neighbouring red-brick rear façades, rather than the overtly modern construction designed by the architect to reflect modern needs and a modern lifestyle.

Party Wall Awards These were required for both the new footings to the extension and the flat above. The process involved negotiations with the neighbours and the owners of the second-floor apartment.

Consultants

The team consisted of the architect, a structural engineer and a party wall surveyor. The client and the architect negotiated costs directly with the contractor.

▲ The existing conservatory extension, seen here, was demolished completely before work began.

Design issues

● The front door of the house is set into a traditional façade, no different from the other houses along the street. To create a modern feel, as one moves through to the rear of the house the tall spaces become increasingly stripped of decoration; the glazed rear elevation of the new extension folds away, orientating the main living spaces of the apartment towards the garden.

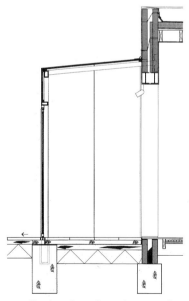

Section through garden extension

Project time in months

Feasibility	Sketch designs		Planning Application			Tender package		Tender out
		1		2	Detail designs	3	4	5	Select contractor

The new extension was designed to be visually separate from the existing house, with a seamless glazed rooflight forming the junction between new and old. The materials (painted rendered blockwork and glass) are also different from those of the existing house, expressing the simple modern language of the interior spaces. There are not many houses in central London that can boast a living room with a ceiling height of almost 4m (12ft) opening onto a 40m (130ft) garden. The space is cool and generous, and lends itself well to long summer parties.

The contract

The client negotiated the contract sum with a single contractor known to him as reliable and capable of producing high-quality finishes. The client did not wish to employ a quantity surveyor and decided to control the costs by using a "Cost Plus" method. With this method, contrary to the usual arrangement, the client pays all the invoices directly, as well as an additional agreed monthly sum to the main contractor. This can make the overall budget difficult to control, but allows the client to be closely involved with the project.

The contractor was not accustomed to working closely with architects who draw every detail, which led to many additional site visits. Nonetheless, the unconventional procurement method worked well on site, was cost effective and produced a well-built and worthwhile end result.

◁ The new rear extension during construction.

▽ The completed rear extension and conservatory. The glazed conservatory doors can fold away, opening the whole of the living room to the large, formal garden.

A study

The client A freelance writer working from home.

The property A large and comfortable Victorian family home, in which the client had carved out a small and cramped workroom off the kitchen.

The brief As the client found that she was spending an increasing amount of time working from home, the inadequacy of her existing study became more apparent and frustrating to her. The architect was initially asked to analyse the house as a whole, to ascertain whether another room might be more appropriate for her needs. In the end the existing space was deemed to be the best for her study. Following this conclusion, the architect was asked to rationalize the room, providing better storage facilities and a more convenient work surface capable of accommodating all necessary equipment, including computer, printer and fax machine.

The architect Barbara Weiss Architects.

▲ Bad storage can negatively affect your efficiency at work. And aesthetics count too!

Administrative issues

There were none.

Consultants

In order to keep professional fees to a minimum, the client requested partial services from the architect, to include design and production drawings, taking the project up to tender stage and appointing the chosen contractor. After that point had been reached, the architect was called in only occasionally, in order to verify that all was proceeding according to plan and to deal with unexpected site events (such as the discovery of dry rot).

Design issues

● The relationship between the kitchen and the study had to be considered carefully, as the client wished to be able to work without interruption even while the kitchen was being used. As the opening between the two spaces is very narrow, a special pivoting door was devised, able to be held back in an open position without intruding on the width of the opening.

● By reducing the area allocated to the hot-water cylinders, the space under the stairs was transformed into a valuable storage slot with access from the study, allowing for a continuous workbench running along three sides of the room. The workbench was finished in a smart yet utilitarian blue-grey lino surface which would survive heavy-duty use.

● The changes in the ceiling levels were

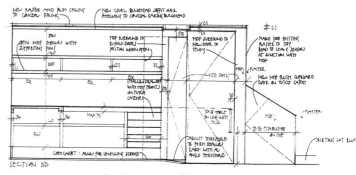

Section showing joinery design

Project time in months

Feasibility	Sketch designs	Detail designs	Tender package	Tender out
		1	2	3

rationalized, providing a greater feeling of order in the room. Low-voltage recessed light fittings were introduced, dramatically improving the atmosphere of the study.

- All wiring and cabling was rationalized, with special cut-outs in the new worktop facilitating connection to various items of equipment.

- The windows looking onto the garden, being neither particularly attractive nor well-positioned, were to be concealed behind the simple lines of a wooden venetian blind. To date, the client has not yet installed this.

- The principal material used for the joinery was MDF, largely painted off-white. The walls, likewise, were painted off-white, and the floor was laid with blue-grey cord carpet.

The contract

The architect sent out a tender package to two small-size builders, both already familiar with the architect's standards of design and workmanship. This was seen as an important issue, as the client anticipated handling all the site operations herself. The contract ran relatively smoothly, although dry rot was discovered in a partition wall at ground-floor level which caused a delay of two weeks as well as substantial extra expense. The contract selected was the JCT Minor Works Agreement.

◁ Once the shell is complete, the plasterer can start his job.

▽ The finished room is functional and cosy, with plenty of well-organized space to store books, stationery and equipment.

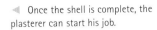

elect contractor	On site		Final tasks	
4		5	6	7

A loft conversion

The client A couple, their daughter aged 9 and their two sons aged 7 and 14.

The property A semi-detached Listed Grade II Regency villa on three floors, situated within an inner city Conservation Area. The neighbour's mirror-image semi-detached house had been extended in the past with an unsightly loft extension on the rear elevation.

The brief The clients wanted to extend their house in order to provide a separate bedroom for each child; it was felt that the elder son needed a room that offered privacy as well as a place to study. The husband's dream was to obtain an extra bathroom with a "proper" shower, while his wife's priority was to increase storage space.

The architect Barbara Weiss Architects.

▲ After completion of the extension, the new loft remains invisible from the garden.

Administrative issues

Planning Permission This was required as the clients had previously extended the house at lower-ground-floor level, using up their "permitted development" allowance. The loft extension did not prove controversial.

Building Regulations Consent The house just complied with fire escape regulations, with the new loft floor precisely within the maximum height off the ground allowed for a new storey.

Listed Building Consent English Heritage was concerned that despite the works the semi-detached pair of houses should remain identical from the street. The neighbour's clumsy rear dormer was disallowed as a precedent as it was felt it would not be permitted today. Eventually a traditional dormer on the rear was agreed, with a larger, more unusual one on the side elevation; the architect had to prove that these would be barely visible from the street. The clients benefited from VAT legislation stipulating minimal tax on works on listed buildings.

Party Wall Awards To avoid being embroiled in party wall issues the structural engineer designed a scheme that did not rely on the party wall to carry the extra floor load. Although this was

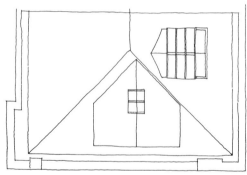

Roof plan

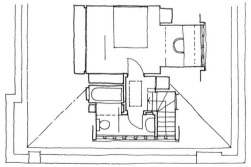

Second-floor plan

Project time in months

Feasibility Sketch designs	1	Planning Application	2		3	Detail designs	4	Tender package	5	Tender out

▲ A musty roof void with adequate headroom can be full of potential.

more complex to design and execute, the savings on fees were greater than the extra expenditure.

Consultants

The team comprised the architect, the structural engineer, and a planning consultant who advised on the negotiations with English Heritage. At the time of selecting a contractor, a firm of quantity surveyors assisted in negotiating a contract sum.

Design issues

● Headroom in the loft was limited; the architect had to establish immediately how much useful floor area could be obtained. The stair between the first and second floors had to be designed with great precision to comply with regulations.
● The final size and position of the dormer windows were a compromise between the clients' wishes and the conservative approach imposed by English Heritage. Extra light was admitted by glazing the roof of the bedroom dormer.
● Temperature control was achieved by using a high level of insulation in the roof void. The two dormers and the opening skylight over the stairs were designed to provide cross-ventilation.
● To reduce noise transmission the architect introduced a floating floor (separating the floorboards from the joists by rubber buffers).
● The areas of the loft with no headroom were exploited for storage; the son's room was "wrapped" in cupboards and shelf units.
● In contrast with the Regency detailing of the house, this floor was designed as modern and clean-lined, with wide plank oak flooring, white walls, and minimal bathroom fittings.

The contract

The clients negotiated a contract sum with a builder known to them, and lived in the house while the extension was being erected. The first phase (the fitting out of the loft space) was carried out with access from the garden, and the knock-through between the floors was done at the very end.

▲ Traditional dormers with a glazed roof proved acceptable to the conservation officer.

◄ A light study/bedroom at the top of the house is every teenager's dream.

A kitchen extension

The client A young couple and their two children, a daughter aged two and a son newly born.

The property A detached five-bedroom, two-reception Edwardian house on two floors plus large attic rooms. The property is soundly built but had been neglected over the years and was in need of repair and refurbishment. A small original rear extension housed the kitchen, with a dilapidated conservatory alongside. The garden is large, around 18m (90ft) long, with rear access and a garage at the end. Construction is stock yellow London brick, a slated roof and sash windows.

The brief The clients had moved from a three-bedroom terraced house with a small patio, wanting more space, a garden and a quiet location. As they both work, one of them partly from home, they needed room for a nanny and a studio. The hall was cramped and dark and needed enlarging. The main requirement, though, was for a large kitchen/diner to replace the existing extension.

Design architect Louis Hellman Architect.
Executive architect Redmond Ivie Architect.

▲ The original rear of the house was slightly dilapidated.
▼ The new extension lends a stylish air to the house.

Administrative issues

Planning Permission The architect calculated that if the existing extensions were demolished they could be replaced with a new kitchen/diner measuring 7 x 6m (23 x 20ft) without needing planning permission, since the additional volume would be within the 70 cubic metres allowed as "permitted development" by the council (the house had never been extended previously). This would avoid the cost, delay and uncertainty involved in a Planning Application. The house is not in a Conservation Area or listed.

Building Regulations Consent A submission was made for the new extension, together with some of the internal reorganization of the house and revised drainage layouts.

Party Wall Awards The clients talked to each of the neighbours and found them friendly and accommodating. Both stated that they had no objection to the proposed extension (similar extensions had been added to each of the neighbours' houses), and this was confirmed informally in writing by the clients.

Programme The clients rented a furnished house and put their furniture into storage until the contract was finished. The schedule had to be tight to minimize this expense.

Project time in months

Feasibility	Sketch designs	Detail designs	Tender package	Tender out
		1	2	3

Consultants

A structural engineer calculated the necessary beam sizes, but a quantity surveyor was not required. The executive architect agreed to make valuations during the contract.

Design issues

• The clients had clear ideas about what they wanted. They required the internal height of the new extension to be near the ceiling height of the existing ground-floor rooms – 3m (10ft). They also wanted café-style french doors out to a paved patio, and daylight provided to the rear rooms giving onto the extension.

• The height requirement presented a design problem, in that the windows to the rear bedrooms made a pitched gable roof difficult. The architect suggested two alternative solutions, of which the clients chose a leaded flat roof with a central lantern (A) and a long rooflight (B) between the extension and the house to give daylight to the rear room and hall.

• For the rear elevation the client opted for a simple screen of piers extending across the whole width of the garden, in facing brick to match the house, with shallow red brick arches to echo the existing sash window openings.

▲ The roof lantern gives extra height and light to the extension and helps to brighten the rear rooms.

• The clients chose the kitchen units and light fittings and the internal finishes of limestone flooring and painted plaster.

The contract

After the tenders were received, a builder who had been recommended by a friend of the clients was awarded the contract in consultation with the architect. He had supplied the lowest tender and had quoted 10 weeks as the time required for building the extension. The work to the existing house was in addition to this.

▼ The airy new kitchen/diner looks towards the garden.

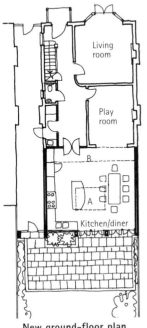

New ground-floor plan

Living room

Play room

B

A

Kitchen/diner

A three-storey extension

The client A couple, both professionals and both requiring work space within the home. At the time of instructing their architect they had a two-year-old daughter and were expecting a baby, who was duly born during the course of the works.

The property A four-storey Regency house at the end of a quiet cul-de-sac, Listed Grade II, with an attached dilapidated low garage and a small three-storey side extension. The house is part of a symmetrical terrace of three houses. The first house in the group, a mirror image of this one, had been extended in the past with a large three-storey side extension. The property enjoys a large, south-facing garden.

The brief The clients saw the opportunity of demolishing the garage and side extension and replacing them with a much larger extension, to match the one at the opposite end of their terrace. Internally, they originally wanted a generous kitchen/family room and a playroom at lower-ground-floor level, which they imagined extending into the garden via a completely glazed and quite modern conservatory. They were also wanting a study and guest cloakroom at upper-ground-floor level, and a new family bathroom and an en suite master bathroom and dressing room at first-floor level. The top floor of the house had been renovated by the clients when they first moved in and accommodated the daughter's room and a guest bathroom.

The architect Barbara Weiss Architects.

▲ Demolishing and rebuilding a narrow side extension is a good way of enlarging and rationalizing your house.

Existing ground-floor plan

Administrative issues

Listed Building Consent English Heritage and the council's conservation officer were adamant that the new extension should be an exact replica of the one at the opposite end of the terrace. As a consequence, the fenestration imposed did not necessarily coincide with the optimum positioning for the layout proposed. In particular, the floor levels in the clients' house did not correspond to those in the one already extended, so windows in the extension were either very high or very low off the ground. The architect resolved the issue by accepting the unusual window locations and accentuating them as an architectural feature in the rooms. During the course of the project, English Heritage had to be consulted over several issues; some were resolved through discussion, but for others it took a specialist historic buildings consultant to persuade English Heritage to allow

Project time in months

Feasibility	Sketch		Planning Application		Detail		Tender package		Tender out		Select con-	
	1	designs	2	3	4	designs	5	6	7	8	tractor	9

◀ While demolition gives way early in the programme to the erection of the new structure, internal finishes are slower to progress.

Consultants

As mentioned, the architects worked with a historic buildings consultant in order to resolve tricky conservation issues. A structural engineer was essential in the design and construction of the new extension, particularly at the interface with the existing house. The services of a quantity surveyor were not considered necessary. The clients took over the initial financial negotiations once the tenders were returned, and then handled the valuations for stage payments with the builder. As the architect to proceed with her design, as in the case of the removal of the staircase to the lower ground floor from its original position to the new extension. The relationship with the conservation department was generally quite fraught, and this delayed progress substantially.

Party Wall Awards As the foundations for the new extension were within 3m (10ft) of the neighbours' wall, the architects served party wall notices on the adjoining owners, who were happy for the work to proceed without bringing in their own party wall surveyor. The architects carried out a detailed photographic survey in order to have on record a schedule of the conditions of the neighbours' house prior to the works.

The excavations caused some minor cracks in the neighbours' stairwell, and the clients agreed to pay their own contractor to carry out the necessary redecorating.

▶ The end product after all the effort; gradual weathering will tone down colour differences in the brick.

relationship with the builder was good through-out the job, this administrative arrangement was a success. In general, however, it would have been safer to stick more closely to the rule book, with the architect performing the cost control tasks as usual.

Design issues

• The architect convinced the clients, after many discussions and three-dimensional sketches, that a very modern, glazed conservatory would be to the detriment of their beautiful Regency rear elevation, as it would cut across the vertical lines of the ornamental brickwork recesses; even more convincingly, while it would prove to be an expensive element in the budget, it would generate very little useful additional space. It was agreed, therefore, that the lower-ground-floor windows would be turned into new french doors opening directly onto the garden, improving dramatically the relationship between indoors and outdoors.

• The architect discussed with the clients their current and envisaged future lifestyle, and persuaded them to add to their brief an independent nanny suite at lower ground floor. This would allow live-in help to co-exist with the family with a relatively small loss of the family's privacy. The family's main living areas were separated from the nanny quarters by the built-in kitchen units and the pantry, which acted as an acoustic buffer blocking noise transmission.

▲ In a tight bathroom clever positioning of mirrors can help to create a feeling of extended space; the reflected light from the window gives a sense of airiness.

• The position of the new stair to the lower ground floor was debated at length and was finally fixed in the new extension.

• In a similar manner, the family room layout as a whole underwent several alterations and revisions. The final arrangement allows for a discreet cooking corner at one end, and an eating and sitting zone in the most visible portion of the room.

• The new playroom volume was extended into the garden, forming a sheltered sun-trap patio for

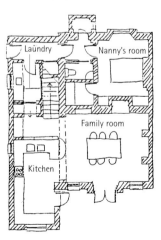

Option 'A' lower ground-floor plan

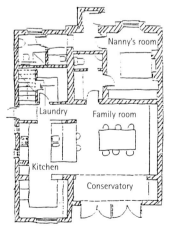

Option 'B' lower ground-floor plan

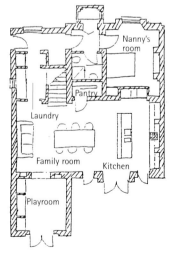

Option 'C', the chosen plan

eating, immediately outside the kitchen. Large toy cupboards form an integral part of the room.

The contract

The selected tenderer was the one who had submitted the lowest price. It was discovered, at a later date, that he had mistakenly not allowed for a whole floor of brickwork, but he absorbed the cost of his mistake without raising the issue with the clients.

Although he was very helpful and willing, the builder's standard of finishes needed careful monitoring at the end of the contract. Most importantly, his ability to complete the job within the dates anticipated left a lot to be desired, as tradesmen were sent to other jobs at the crucial conclusion point of this job. As the clients had moved into rented accommodation at the outset of the works, and had recently had another child, the ever-fluctuating moving-in date caused them much annoyance.

However, on the whole, the project ran relatively smoothly. The clients were very enthusiastic and hands-on in their approach.

◀◀ The repositioned and carefully detailed staircase is a gracious main feature in the house.

◀ A glass and steel balustrade visually opens up the study to the floor below.

▼ The new family room is the focus of the house. Its enhanced relationship with the garden was viewed as the key to the success of this space.

A flat conversion

The client A couple, both involved in the fashion world, and their son aged 16 and daughter aged 14.

The property A 200m² flat on the fifth floor of an early 1970s award-winning block. The flat had been occupied by an elderly lady, who had added Corinthian columns to the dining room and egg-and-dart cornices throughout. The furnishings generally were tired and out of keeping with the original design intent of the building. The ceilings were relatively low, and the windows needed replacing. The maid's suite was redundant.

The brief The clients were moving from a Victorian house to the flat, in search of a more urban, stylish life. They particularly welcomed being on the fifth floor, with fewer security anxieties. They requested three bedrooms, three bathrooms and a guest cloakroom, a study/dressing room, a living room, a dining room, a kitchen and a laundry room. The daughter's room should be large enough to double up as a sitting room/study, and the son's room needed to accommodate his hi-fi equipment. Generally, storage was an important issue.

The architect Barbara Weiss Architects.

Administrative issues

Permits According to the lease, permission had to be sought for all works from the building management. In particular, any replacement windows had to conform to the management's guidelines. Having investigated alternative procurement routes, the architect suggested that the client use the same subcontractor who had replaced the majority of the building's windows.

Building Regulations Consent It became apparent very early on that, in order to meet the fire regulations, it would be necessary to provide a secondary escape route from the bedroom wing. This was achieved by creating a door within a false kitchen unit, allowing a possible escape via the kitchen on to the access balcony and service

stair core. This arrangement was not entirely satisfactory from a purely architectural point of view, largely owing to the loss of valuable storage space, but proved to be a reasonable compromise acceptable to both the clients and the Building Control Officer.

Programme The neighbour downstairs was uncooperative during the course of the works, complaining about noise levels and insisting on more than one occasion that construction should be halted. The delays caused by her had serious repercussions on the builders' progress.

Consultants

The architect had previously worked on the fitting-out of the clients' fashion showroom, so the two parties knew each other's style and working practices well. This familiarity significantly helped to speed up the design process, as mutual likes and dislikes were acknowledged at an early stage by

Existing floor plan

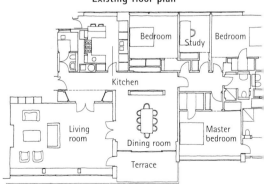

New floor plan

Project time in months

Feasibility	Sketch designs	Detail designs	Tender package		Tender out	Select c
	1	2	3	4	5	tractor

▲ Sometimes a lot of imagination is needed to visualize the potential of an unmodernized property.

▼ The same room as above – after "the treatment".

On site | | | | | Final tasks | |
| 7 | 8 | 9 | 10 | 11 | 12 |

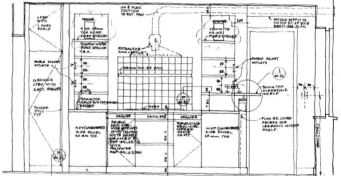

▲ The kitchen, as originally found, was bland in design and noticeably "tired". A complete rethink was required.

▷ While no bigger than it used to be, the new kitchen is light and elegant, with a place for everything.

Section through kitchen

both parties. For structural advice the architect referred back to the engineers who had originally constructed the building and who still had at their disposal copies of their original drawings.

On completion of the project the clients requested assistance from an interior decorator, who helped them in the purchase of the most suitable furniture for the new rooms. Although this process took a comparatively long period of time, ultimately the very elegant end result justified the delay. Furnishing a new environment is another important design process which cannot be rushed if it is to be successful.

Design issues

• The spine walls were originally constructed in reinforced concrete, making their demolition virtually impossible. This condition, coupled with the presence of service ducts for the whole building running through the flat in specific locations, caused major constraints on the plan form of the new layout.

• The large picture windows determined the size of the rooms, offering little flexibility in the plan. Owing to this, and to the factors described above, planning the circulation around the flat was occasionally awkward, as structural conditions often interfered with obvious entry points into a room.

• The clients had bought the property with a few, very precise ideas for the overall "look" of the flat. In particular, the bathroom finishes and marbles were to be more or less copies of ones encountered in hotels abroad. For the master bathroom the architect was asked to design according to the spirit of photographs supplied by the clients. In other areas, however, the clients were much more tentative, leaving to the architect the task of inspiring them with ideas for possible alternative finishes.

• The clients asked the architect to reuse several of the interior carcasses of the existing cupboards and to incorporate them in the new storage units created in all the bedrooms.

• The kitchen was designed to maximize the food preparation area, and also to include a bar for informal eating. The decision to display glasses and certain other objects was balanced by a very precise brief for the concealment of less interesting kitchen implements.

The contract

Several tenders were received back. In the end the clients decided to appoint once again the builders who had recently completed the refurbishment of their fashion showroom – despite the fact that they were not the cheapest tenderers –

▶ The original bathrooms were old-fashioned and lacked style.

▼ Marble in large quantities gives a feeling of luxury – the perfect material for a bathroom in which to pamper oneself.

because they knew them and had been pleased with the quality of their work.

The works were run under the JCT Minor Works Agreement and ran fairly smoothly, although there was an overrun of six weeks. Unconvinced by the contractors' budget costs for certain items, the clients decided to specify and source their own sanitary ware and timber parquet floors, believing they could make savings this way. However, as the architect predicted might happen, the main contractor was delayed in the installation of the bathroom fittings, owing to the supplier's not producing the goods at the right point. The standard of finish of the parquet flooring was also found by the architect to be patchy and generally unsatisfactory. Both these elements proved the point that, however appealing the idea, it is not advisable to short-cut the main contractor by supplying materials and services outside the main contract, as the architect loses control and the delays often cost more than any savings achieved by taking this route.

A town-house conversion

The client A writer and an architectural historian, both in their late twenties.

The property The clients had purchased an old shop, originally a cobbler's, latterly used as a design studio, in extremely decrepit condition. The property had an open ground-floor space with an ugly metal staircase leading to two rooms on the first floor. This lower level had a kitchenette and shower room within an oddly shaped area that had originally been the back yard. The main space was paved with engineering brick, and a partition had been erected almost immediately behind the front window.

The brief The clients' brief was to replan and rehabilitate the building to provide accommodation appropriate to their specific needs on a limited budget. The property would, ideally, provide a room for each of them to work at home, areas for living and entertaining, and some outdoor space.

The architect Alastair Howe Architects.

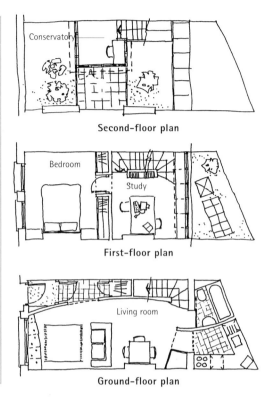

Second-floor plan

First-floor plan

Ground-floor plan

Administrative issues

Planning Permission Although the property (which is located in a Conservation Area) had been sold with the benefit of planning permission for a change of use from commercial to residential, it was necessary to obtain further planning consent for the addition of a conservatory and roof terrace on the top of the property. An application was submitted, and consent was gained after some minor amendments to ensure that the roof works would not be visible from street level.

Building Regulations Consent Once planning permission had been granted, an application for consent under the Building Regulations was made. Owing to the additional room on the roof, consideration had to be given to protecting the route down to ground level from significant fire risk. Because of the limited available space, the design required that the stair be open to the ground-floor space, so it would not be a

"protected route" to outside. In fact the authority accepted that, in the event of a fire, escape would be possible from the upper floors across the roofs of adjoining properties.

Party Wall Awards Party wall notices were issued to the owners of the adjoining properties, who eventually agreed to the proposals. The architect initially submitted the notices, but, as negotiations became less than straightforward, he advised the clients to engage a party wall surveyor to give specialist advice.

Consultants

In addition to the architect, the clients employed a structural engineer and a party wall surveyor.

Design Issues

• The design of the new house evolved over a number of informal meetings between the architect and the clients, and in due course the final design was agreed. Owing to the location

Project time in months

Feasibility	Sketch designs 1	Planning Application Detail designs 2	Tender package 3	Tender out 4	Select contractor 5

of existing services (such as drainage) and the limited space and budget, it was decided to retain the kitchen and the bathroom in the rear yard area. The bathroom makes the most of the oddly shaped narrow end of the old yard to shoehorn in a bath, lavatory and basin. The larger end of the yard was turned over to the kitchen, and the distant, least accessible corner was used to house the boiler.

● By using curves in the plan the space was made highly efficient, and the penetration of some kitchen appliances to the living area was barely noticeable.

● The whole of the old yard area was covered with a glazed roof to allow maximum light to the kitchen and bathroom. The theme of curves was carried through the living space, where a gently curved wall conceals a coat cupboard and a new stair to the first floor. This wall was punctured to allow more light to the rear of the living area from the light first-floor area.

● Upstairs the stair wraps around a bookcase in the rear room, which became a study. The stair to the second floor became an open-tread stair in contrast to the

◀ This view of the ground floor prior to the work shows the spiral stair and the doors to the kitchenette and shower room.

▼ After the work, the new stair rises behind the yellow wall; the openings in the back wall were kept so as to reduce structural work.

closed-tread stair to the first floor. Again, this was to allow more light down to lower levels.

- A new conservatory was positioned on the roof, against one neighbour's raised party wall.
- Because all three floors are interconnected, and heat rises, an elementary air recirculation device consisting of a duct and a fan was utilized to take warm air back to the ground floor from the top of the building.
- The clients were keen to experiment with the use of bright colours: the front door is purple, the study floor bright blue, and the walls yellow, green and red.

The contract

While the application for Building Regulations Consent was being considered by the local authority, the project was tendered to a number of builders. When tenders were returned, all were higher than the original budget for the work. Negotiations ensued with the two lowest tenderers and a number of items were revised or omitted; eventually the lowest tenderer was

engaged on a JCT Minor Works Agreement and work was begun. As the existing structure was opened up it was found that work had been carried out by previous owners in a far from satisfactory manner. The roof was a particular case in point: even though several exploratory holes had been made in the ceiling prior to tenders being invited, none had exposed the terrible condition of most of the roof, which necessitated an almost entirely new roof structure. As the job progressed it transpired that the contractors had underpriced much of the work; however, the job was finally completed successfully after many lengthy and convoluted debates between architect and contractors on costs for variations and extra constructional issues.

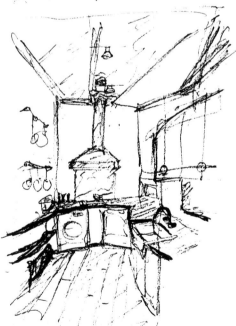

▲ The sketch proposal for the kitchen shows how all the details are planned to fit neatly so as to make the most of the small space.

◀ As work progresses in the kitchen the sketch gradually starts to become reality.

▶ The kitchen is finally complete.

▲ The view into the bathroom, with the kitchen to the right, demonstrates the vibrant use of colour.

▶ The stairs to the second floor wrap around a bookcase.

▼ From the study room open-tread stairs (seen on left) ascend to the second floor, allowing light from the large existing window to filter down to the room below.

A rural conversion

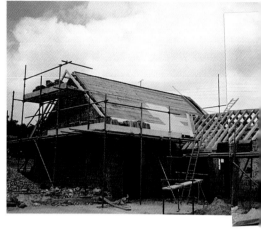

The client A well-established property developer; the project was the responsibility of one of its directors.

The property The setting is a sloping basin of land with a roadside edge and views of farmland on all sides. The existing property consisted of three derelict 19th-century dairy buildings, each single-storeyed, stone-walled and roofed with clay tiles. Opposite the site is the old farmhouse, now occupied by a wood-craftsman and his family. Nearby are two barns, one of which serves as the wood-craftsman's workshop and the other as shelter for the adjoining farm's cattle.

The brief The architect's initial feasibility study established the need to renovate the existing buildings in order to repair damage to them. It also investigated the options available to the client in terms of developing the site. From this study a number of options were presented regarding various mixes of use for the property, together with issues regarding the loan payback period. A brief was then formulated, based on the chosen option, to convert and extend the buildings and adjoining external areas so as to provide two craft workshops and one lettable holiday unit together with parking requirements.

The architect Sergison Bates Architects.

Administrative issues

Planning Permission The site is in an area of Outstanding Natural Beauty, and so careful discussion was needed with the local planning authority. Planning permission was required for the change of use of the buildings. Initial discussions with the authority established that a mix of work and holiday let would be looked upon favourably. All external alterations, including the extension for the holiday let, required planning permission. The treatment of the elevations and the careful choice of materials persuaded the planners to grant permission.

Building Regulations Consent The different types of use meant that one-hour fire separation had to be introduced between the workshops and the holiday let. The small scale of the workshops and the few people who would work there meant

Project time in months

Feasibility	Sketch designs	Planning Application		Detail designs	Tender package			Tender
1	2	3	4	5	6	7	8	9

▲ The entire roof was stripped to permit repairs to the timbers and to allow the tiles to be cleaned.

▲ The central cowsheds became the second studio.

Studio 2

Studio 1

Lettable holiday unit

Floor plan

that consent was straightforward. The roofs to all the existing buildings, together with the walls to the holiday let, were upgraded thermally by the addition of insulation to the inside. An entire new underground drainage system was installed, the details of which had to be agreed on site with the Building Control surveyor.

Environment Agency Consent A new sewage treatment plant and soakaway were installed to deal with the sewage from the development. These required a Permission to Discharge. A detailed survey had to be carried out, investigating all nearby waterways (rivers, streams, culverts), and plans locating them had

to be submitted. Since the proposal was to replace the existing 50-year-old soakaway, consent was easily gained.

Highways Consent The new car park entrance needed consent from the local Highways Department. Drawings were submitted, and negotiations were held with the area inspector to agree sightlines, materials and so on.

Consultants

The team comprised the architect, a structural engineer and a heating engineer. Because the project was subject to the requirements of the Construction (Design and Management)

▲ The relationship between kitchen and living room can be adjusted via the two double doors.

◀ For speed of construction, metal supports were used to make the spaces in the holiday let.

Regulations, the appointment of a planning supervisor was required. The firm of architects was qualified to offer this service.

Design issues

• Each of the three buildings forming the dairy was assigned a use. Two made the studio spaces, while the third, extended to double its original area, provided for the holiday unit.

• Three external spaces were made, each with its own relationship to the buildings and the farmland. The first was a gravelled car parking area which would also serve as a place to deliver materials to the workshop; the second was a working yard for the craft studios and included a new timber-framed outbuilding with translucent roof panels, while the third was a garden to the holiday unit, bounded by hedge and a raised earth border, with views out to farmland and beyond. Each of these areas was formed by terracing the sloping landscape and was defined by new timber fences with staggered boarding.

• In the craft studios the existing construction was slightly modified and tuned (added insulation, exposed services, window frames, concrete floor) so that the construction of stone wall and timber roof remained as a background.

• In the holiday unit the existing construction became a shell, being hidden by the insulated plasterboard linings of the walls and of the variously angled ceilings. The linings extended into the new construction, connecting the new with the old. Lighting was incorporated as part of the lining, with opal polycarbonate panels laid flush with the plasterboard.

• New cedar cladding in the form of rainscreen boarding or louvres was fixed to one or more faces of the buildings. The louvres screen large areas of glazing set back from the façades, giving a richly layered assembly. The cedar was treated differently, from rough-sawn to planed and smooth, depending on its location. All the materials used externally – cedar, mill-finish aluminium, grey roofing felt and Douglas fir plywood – were chosen to weather to a silver grey to match the existing stone.

The contract

Three contractors were invited to tender for the project, each of whom was investigated in terms of referees and previous work. Of the two offering the lowest prices, one was a small family firm, the other a much larger company. The architect felt that, given the nature of the project, the smaller builders were more suitable, and made this recommendation to the client.

Because the site was empty the contract (a JCT Minor Works Agreement) was not complex. It was agreed at the start of work on site where the contractor could park vehicles and store materials to avoid disruption to the neighbours, although it is advisable to specify these arrangements in the tender documents. Repair of the existing building proved more extensive than had been envisaged, as it had deteriorated considerably over the winter prior to construction. A disused well was also discovered, which the client wanted to bring back into use. The costs of both these areas were in addition to the contract sum and were agreed in accordance with the terms of the contract.

The project has proved very successful: the workshops were pre-let, and the holiday let has now established itself as a unique place to stay.

▲ The untreated cedar has now weathered almost to silver, a colour similar to the old stone of the buildings.

▼ The finished project has given new life to the otherwise redundant farm buildings.

A self-build house

"Self-build" is a broad term covering building works with a wide spectrum of owner involvement, ranging from input into the design process, through management of the contracting process, to the physical labour of building. Although the house described here was designed and built by an architect and his family, many of the issues involved are the same for a layperson embarking on the self-build route.

The owner The couple, an architect and a teacher, with a 2-year-old daughter, were first-time buyers searching for a suitable property but unable to find anything that satisfied their criteria. They had vaguely considered self-build, and then several plots became available in the locality.

The property The couple put in an offer on a plot that was being marketed as a "self-build plot" with planning consent for a kit home, but their offer was not accepted, and they were told that someone else had offered the full asking price. However, some time later the original plot came back on the market, and this time, with funding and a sketch proposal in mind, they were successful in purchasing the land.

The brief The brief was simply for a very economical but interesting family home.

The cost The total cost of the project was split almost evenly between the building work (48%) and the cost of the site (52%) – a high relative proportion owing to the location. The owners estimate that the building work would probably have cost more than half as much again for a layperson, who would have had to allow for architect's and other fees and perhaps would not have done so much of the physical labour. However, the completed house was valued at substantially more than its cost to build, so the self-build route could still offer good value to those suited to in-depth involvement in the construction of their own home.

The architect Alastair Howe Architects.

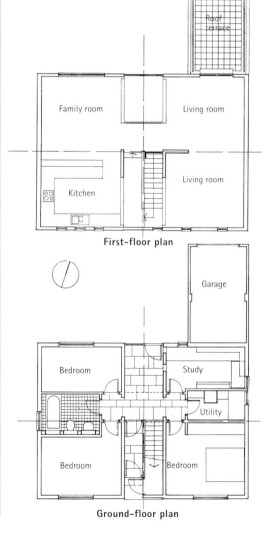

First-floor plan

Ground-floor plan

Project time in months

Feasibility		Sketch designs	Planning Application			Detail designs		Tender out
	1		**2**		**3**	**4**	Tender package	**5** On site

◁ The concrete blockwork structure to the ground floor is built.

△ The structure is ready for external insulation and render.

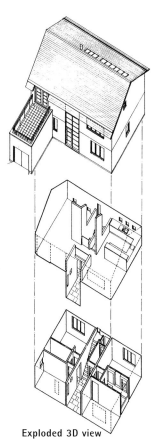

Exploded 3D view

◁ The view of the completed rear elevation shows the carefully positioned windows, with traditional stained black frames.

Administrative issues

Planning Permission Having made an initial offer on the building plot, the future owners were spurred into designing a house for the site. They consulted the local planners – who declared themselves "cautiously supportive" of the design – and, with a friendly builder, prepared budget costings. The couple then put these costings to one of the high-street banks, in search of funding. The bank manager agreed to support an application for a self-build mortgage; this would provide funds for 90 per cent of the land purchase and would then release further payments at stages during the building of the house. Once their offer for the plot had been accepted, the owners immediately submitted a Planning Application that was a development of the earlier sketch proposals. Although the plot had been sold with planning permission for a dwelling, a new application was needed because the house that the couple wanted to build was significantly different. In due course, and after a number of small modifications to alleviate neighbours' concerns – mainly regarding potential problems of overlooking – planning permission was granted.

Consultants

The only additional consultant on the project was a structural engineer.

▲ Development sketch of entrance hall and stair with bridge over.

◀ This view from the head of the stairs looks towards the bridge and double-height entrance screen.

Design issues

• The design of the house was specific both to the requirements of the family and to the site. The plot was one of four with consent for cottage-style kit houses, and was at the end of a row of 1970s speculatively built houses. There is a view over rising farmland to the front, and to the rear other houses are about 50m (160ft) away.

• The house was designed "upside down" – that is, with the living accommodation on the upper floor – using the roof volume to gain a generous feeling of space, and taking advantage of the views across the farmland.

• To the rear, careful positioning of small windows ensured that views of the garden were maintained while overlooking of the neighbouring properties was avoided.

• The garage roof to the front of the house was utilized as an outdoor area directly off the first-floor living area.

• Bedrooms and ancillary accommodation were located on the ground floor, with the double-height entrance hall connecting this floor with the living accommodation above. The stairs lead directly up to the living space from under a bridge to which one returns after passing a slit window with views of the back garden.

• Materials for the building were kept as simple as possible. The structure is mainly timber-framed for maximum strength in the long spanning walls and roof at first floor. The walls are externally insulated and coated with a white render and the window frames black-stained to reflect the local vernacular. The mass of the house is similar to the 1970s houses next door, thus creating a kind of "bridge" between them and the cottagey houses on the other side.

• Internally the walls are painted plaster. The roof is lined with ply for structural reasons, although the birch-faced type was used for aesthetic reasons.

• Simple services (hot and cold water and underfloor heating) completed the design.

The contract

Once planning permission was granted, the owners prepared a series of very specific drawings of all the construction aspects of the house with which to gain prices for the work to be done. These were somewhat different from the drawings that an architect would prepare for a "traditional" procurement method, where a single contractor would coordinate all the work. The basic difference was that, instead of showing the building as an effectively finished article, each drawing related to a specific trade or operation, such as foundations, concrete blockwork, timber framing and walls. There were two reasons for this approach: first, the drawings were able to be priced by individual tradespeople (the owners acting as the main contractor); and secondly, this allowed them to measure accurately the quantities of materials required and to order these from individual suppliers at the best prices.

Once construction started, there followed five months of intense hard work with many emotional highs and lows. The couple spent a lot of time obtaining quotes and placing orders, and also visited site regularly. Once works had reached a point where DIY was possible, they did much of the physical work, with family help.

◀ The clean, simple shape of the front of the house becomes dramatic when the lights come on after dark.

▼ The roof height gives the first-floor living area a spacious, airy feel. The kitchen is on the left below the rooflights; in the foreground is the void to the entrance hall.

A new-build house

The client A young single businessman, living in a large listed Georgian house in a London square.

The property A derelict garage at the back of the client's garden, with access from the mews. The site is set within a Conservation Area, although the houses fronting onto the mews are all shapes and sizes and in several different architectural styles, from Victorian to Modernist. In this area the gardens between houses are quite short, as the mews have substantially eaten into them.

The brief While keen to develop the site at the end of the garden, the client initially could not decide whether to build the largest possible house the planners would allow or a smaller, more unobtrusive structure that would not spoil the enjoyment of his garden when it was looked at from his own house opposite. Eventually, after a few superseded Planning Applications submitted to explore the planners' responses, it was agreed that a two-bedroom house on three floors would fit the bill. Ideally the completed house would be rented out to a young professional couple or to older people wanting a *pied-à-terre* in the city. The layout therefore had to be fairly flexible, as the end users' precise requirements could only be guessed. The client insisted that the second bedroom should double up as a study, and that the reception areas be generous so that the tenants could entertain in comfort.

The architect Barbara Weiss Architects.

▲ A small site needs to be run efficiently, as storage space for materials is limited. Hoarding protects neighbours' gardens from dust and helps to reduce noise.

Administrative issues

Planning Permission The planners insisted that the client provide two off-street car parking spaces, one to replace the garage that was currently serving the main house and one for the new house. This requirement had great impact on the design of the house, as the ground floor was largely eaten up by a one-car garage. The second off-street car parking space was to be provided on the garage forecourt. The planners were also very concerned about the overall massing of the new house and its compliance with existing adjoining set-backs and general street lines. These restrictions determined to a large extent the overall imprint of the house on the ground. At the rear of the house the planners ruled that terraces would not be allowed and that all windows had to be above eye level or glazed with translucent – not transparent – glass, to avoid overlooking of other properties. The materials to be used on the external elevations were also vetted carefully, to fit in with the surrounding buildings. Ironically, the houses on both sides underwent major transformations during the erection of the client's house (one was demolished and rebuilt in a Modernist style, the other was painted black), so, by the date of completion, the client's house appeared to stand out in the street far more than it was intended to.

Landscaping The garden at the rear contained a magnolia protected by a Tree Preservation Order; the architect had to negotiate with the council's arboriculturalist regarding the treatment of the root ball of the tree and the distance between it and the new structure. Despite several meetings and lots of correspondence aimed at protecting it, the neighbours' contractors managed to kill

Project time in months

Feasibility	Sketch designs	Planning Application			Detail designs	Tender package		Tender out
1	2	3	4		5	6	7	8	9

Street elevation

▲ A Conservation Area can accommodate a variety of architectural styles, as long as guidelines for height and massing are respected.

▶ The composition of windows and doors provides a distinctive identity for this building.

▼ As the walls go up, the project becomes an exciting reality.

off the tree during the course of their works to the house next door.

Party Wall Awards Originally the structural engineer conceived sharing the southern external flank wall with the neighbouring house, in order to maximize the internal space. It became apparent, though, that it would be very difficult to use the same foundations without underpinning, so the issue was resolved by building another flank wall parallel with the neighbours' but fully within the client's property. On the northern side, party wall matters were more straightforward. However, a dispute arose as to the finish for the dividing flank wall at roof level, as the architect wanted to keep the brick visible and the neighbours wanted to render it, in keeping with their elevation. Eventually the architect achieved the desired finish.

Consultants

The client relied on the architect and a structural engineer. The services were designed by the contractor, based on a strict performance specification set out by the architect. This proved to be problematic, as the subcontractor's design did not meet standards and a lot of trouble-shooting had to take place once the occupier had moved in. A party wall surveyor was appointed to deal with Party Wall Awards.

Design issues

● The orientation of the house (the street side faced west) and the inability to have usable windows on the garden side to a certain extent dictated the overall layout, so that the main rooms were located overlooking the street, and the service rooms at the back. Because of the need for a garage, the second bedroom/study was the only habitable room placed on the garden side, slightly sunk into an open area below the level of the garden.

● The client required a balcony outside the dressing room, conceived to enable future occupiers to sit outside, drinks in hand. The client and the architect spent much time discussing the best way to bring sun and light into the house; this was achieved by introducing a variety of large and small windows throughout the house, largely of traditional design, complemented by skylights on the top floor.

● The architect designed each room to have a distinct personality, whether by playing with the

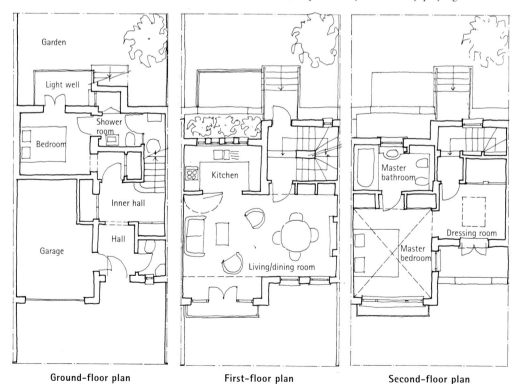

Ground-floor plan   First-floor plan   Second-floor plan

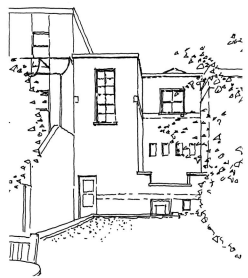

▲ Perspectives help to explore the three-dimensional relationships between the various elements of a building.

▼ With well-considered ergonomic decisions, natural materials and good lighting, the available space in the small kitchen is exploited to the full.

ceiling levels, introducing imaginative joinery items, or framing views in a variety of ways. Notably, the master bedroom enjoys a large, arched, floor-to-ceiling window and a "tented" ceiling that dramatically increases the volume of the room.

● Storage issues were considered carefully, with appropriate cupboards provided for each room.

● Materials were kept natural and durable throughout. The exterior of the house is clad in second-hand London stock brick, similar to that used on the client's house in the adjoining Georgian square. As it was intended that the house was to be rented out, it was agreed that internal finishes should look expensive but in reality be reasonable in cost. A few special elements were therefore dotted around the house to provide a luxury feel, such as the terrazzo vanity unit in the master bathroom, the oak treads on the stair and the oak floors throughout. Maintenance of the house was discussed in detail, as the client was concerned that his

▲ The cast green terrazzo basin brings a note of frivolity to the master bathroom.

investment should not be permanently damaged if a succession of different tenants inhabited it. In the end it was agreed that painted joinery and walls seemed to offer the best chance to renew the original freshness of the town house periodically, after each tenancy.

• Given the size of the site, and the spatial gymnastics required to provide all the accommodation needed, the structural engineer ended up producing a substantially more expensive structural design than would have normally been necessary for a house of this size. This was felt to be a worthwhile expense, as every inch of the house has been made to work.

The contract

The tender package included a complete set of drawings and a National Building Specification, a hefty and comprehensive document that leaves nothing to chance. At the time this was seen by the architect as appropriate for the scale of the job. With hindsight, however, it was found that the small contractors approached for the project were slightly intimidated by the sheer volume of the paperwork, and submitted more expensive tenders than they might have done had they been issued with a less formidable specification.

▲ The stairs leading from the entrance level to the reception floor have oak treads that float above the white risers.

▼ In the master bedroom, a unit with a variety of drawer sizes allows for storing a multitude of items.

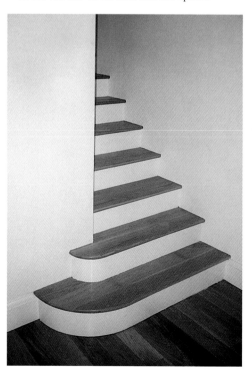

As a result the architect had to spend quite a substantial amount of time negotiating a contract sum acceptable to the client with the tenderers.

A medium-size contractor, known to the architect, was eventually selected and performed satisfactorily in terms of overall quality. The contract overran substantially, partly because the site agent was absent on family matters for a prolonged period, during which the contractors could not find an adequate replacement. An IFC84 form of contract (see p.59) was used.

Upon the completion of the works, the client was so happy with the new house that he decided to move into it himself!

◁ Once the roof is on, the finishing of the interiors is made much easier. With its dramatic arched windows and high, "tented" ceiling the master bedroom enjoys a great feeling of space.

▽ Full-height windows allow lots of light to enter, but the lower section must be fixed shut to prevent accidents.

Cast of characters

architect See pp.14–17.

clerk of works This player is only required if the job is particularly large, or if the site is not local to the architect and, as a consequence, site inspections are rare. A clerk of works is a paid agent of the owner (see **client**). His or her job is to monitor the works on a regular basis and to report any problems back to the architect for comment. In other words, a clerk of works acts as the "eyes" of the owner, a constant and vigilant presence on site that can help to reduce delays and avoid any possible errors.

client Owner of the property, the client is the employer of the architect, of all subsequent consultants required, of the main contractor, and of a clerk of works, if required.

conditions surveyor Typically instructed by the client prior to the purchase of a property, a surveyor will inspect the house in depth and write up a report detailing the conditions of the existing fabric and suggesting essential and non-essential improvements. The level of detail of the report varies considerably according to the level of service that has been agreed at the outset (full structural report, partial report), so make sure you know what you are getting. Note also that surveyors are very adept at covering themselves for not detecting latent defects such as dry rot, woodworm, damaged drains and so on that cannot be seen with the naked eye. It is strongly advisable therefore to use a reputable firm of surveyors, if possible recommended by someone in the know.

interior designer While most architects will argue that good architecture does not require further "dressing up", some clients prefer to bring into the team a specialist who has a particular expertise in fabrics, curtains, colours and furniture. Beware that you do not end up with an architectural hybrid, if your architect and your interior designer are not compatible. It is extremely important that the two should work together with you and complement each other. (See "Choosing your Architect" (pp.18–20) for the selection of an interior designer.) Get your architect to agree to any appointment at an early stage.

party wall surveyor This expert is required when your project involves work to a party wall or to foundations adjacent to your neighbours'. The work you are intending to carry out might have negative consequences on adjoining buildings (perhaps by causing cracks or ruining decorations). Your party wall surveyor will survey your property and the neighbours' and make a photographic record of the existing situation. This will help to determine fairly at the end whether your building works have caused any damage. Your surveyor will also "serve notice" on the neighbours that you intend to carry out work and agree the basis on which they will be compensated if they do suffer damage. The neighbours may instruct their own surveyors to monitor the course of the works, although in such cases you will be obliged to pay everyone's fees. Party wall matters are very expensive. It may be useful to investigate alternative structural solutions that would avoid involving the party wall, even if such solutions are more complex, as this could save you a significant amount of money.

planning consultant If your property, or what you are intending to do to it, causes you very unusual or apparently insoluble planning problems, it may be worth bringing on board a planning consultant. This person will be well-versed in planning policy and procedure and will know how to present your arguments to unwilling bureaucrats in the most convincing way, find legal loopholes, invoke precedents, and generally blind the other side with science. In the case of a planning appeal you will almost certainly need a planning consultant to prepare your case and fight your corner.

quantity surveyor This consultant monitors and advises on costs throughout the project, and is recommended for jobs in excess of £100,000; the fees may well be recovered in the savings that can be obtained on the cost of the works. A QS will analyse the architect's scheme and produce a provisional budget estimate for the works prior to going out for tender, thus alerting the team in the early stages to the possible risk of over-expenditure. He or she will also assist in preparing the tender documents, including producing the Bills of Quantities for larger jobs, analyse the returned tenders and advise on the selection of a contractor. During the course of the works on site a QS will regularly assess and value the amount of work carried out by the builders, thus establishing precisely the size of the payment due from you, the employer. Once the works are completed a QS will agree with the builders the value of the final account, particularly the costs of the variations (additions and omissions) that have occurred during the course of the contract.

services engineer This consultant is necessary if you have particular technical requirements in the areas of heating, lighting, telecommunications, plumbing or drainage, or if you are very interested in "green" issues. He or she can design

sophisticated systems to suit your precise needs and wishes. If you do not use a services engineer for these tasks, your architect can most likely specify a standard system that will be adequate but not technically sophisticated. Design input will possibly be needed from the builders, and your architect will explain how this will be handled contractually. As with the structural engineer, a services engineer will design, calculate, submit drawings to the council, attend site, monitor costs and so on, for this area of expertise.

structural engineer The level of input of a structural engineer depends on the complexity and scale of a project, although one is required on most jobs. An SE analyses existing structural conditions, spotting inherent defects (such as subsidence, rotting beams, weak roof structure); advises the architect on the feasibility of structural changes; and designs new structural elements to suit the architect's plans (lintels over new doors or windows, strengthening of floors, repositioning of roof elements in loft conversions and so on). He or she will also submit calculations for structural work to Building Control, attend site meetings to inspect structural work carried out, and advise on structural costs.

surveyor Although the measured survey (see p.31) might be carried out by the architect (for an extra fee), this can also be done by a surveyor. It is important, however, that the architect should liaise directly with the surveyor and agree the level of information required on the survey. A survey takes approximately two to three weeks to produce, depending on the size of the property. As it is the most essential tool to enable the architect to get started on the design, organizing the measured survey is one of the first things you should address as soon as you have appointed your architect.

How to read drawings

The basic method of communicating building design is by drawings depicting plans, sections and elevations, "read" together, and by reducing the scale of the area or object shown. For laypeople, architects may also use other devices such as perspective drawings or bird's eye views.

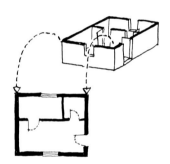

ARCHITECT'S DRAWING

Hellman

The plan

Plans are the equivalent of slicing horizontally through a building at each floor to show as many features as possible: walls, windows, doors, openings, fittings etc. Walls are shown in heavy line, windows and fittings in thinner line. Doors are shown as quarter circle 'door swings', the path taken by the door as it opens fully. Site plans are small scale, like Ordnance Survey maps, whereas room layouts are large scale. Roof plans show the building from above, looking straight down. A "north point" shows the building's orientation.

The section

Sections are the equivalent of slicing vertically through a building at various points to show as many features as possible; they may be taken widthways or lengthways. As with plans, walls are shown in heavy line. Larger-scale sections may show internal elevations of doors, windows and fittings.

The elevation

Elevations are drawings of each face of the building, shown to scale. Larger-scale elevations show more detail, such as brickwork, roof tiles and opening parts of windows. Elevations are normally labelled according to their orientation – "south elevation" indicates that the elevation faces south – relating to the north point on the plan.

North (front) elevation   West (side) elevation

Scale

Scales miniaturize the size of the building drawn. The usual scales are: 1:100 (1cm (½in) on the drawing is equivalent to 1m (3ft) of the building), used for Planning Applications or basic design; 1:50 (2cm (¾in) is equivalent to 1m), used for working drawings or layouts; 1:20 (5cm (2in) is equivalent to 1m), for room layouts; and 1:5 (20cm (8in) is equivalent to 1m), for technical details. Architects have scale rulers off which you can automatically read the relevant dimensions. The scale is usually to be found in the bottom right hand corner of the drawing.

I to 50   I to 100

Index

Acknowledgments

The authors and publishers would like to thank the following for their contribution to the projects: Alastair Howe, Stephen Bates, Mark Tuff, Marston Properties, Michal Cohen, and the clients of the properties illustrated.

Contact details

Barbara Weiss Architects
4 Offord Street
London N1 1DH
Tel 0171 609 1867
Fax 0171 700 2952

Louis Hellman Architect
  (designer)
Redmond Ivie Architect
  (executive architect)
6 Montague Gardens
London W3 9PT
Tel/Fax 0181 992 8318

Alastair Howe Architects
50 Tanners Way
Hunsdon Ware
Herts SG12 8QF
Tel 01279 843936
Fax 01279 843937

Sergison Bates Architects
44 Newman Street
London W1P 3PA
Tel 0171 255 1564
Fax 0171 636 5646

Walters and Cohen
2nd Floor, Block E
Carkers Lane
53–79 Highgate Road
London NW5 1TL
Tel 0171 428 9751
Fax 0171 428 9752

Useful addresses

RIBA Client Advisory Service
66 Portland Place
London W1N 4AD
Tel 0171 307 3700
Fax 0171 436 9112

The Architecture Foundation
30 Bury Street
London SW1Y 6AU
Tel 0171 839 9389
Fax 0171 839 9380
(events and exhibitions)

Picture acknowledgments

Alastair Howe Architects 96, 97 centre, 97 bottom, 98 centre left, 98 centre right, 98 bottom right, 99 top right, 104 top, 104 centre, 104 bottom, 105 right, 105 top, 105 centre, 106 right, 107 bottom
Anne Price 84 top
Helen Binet 102 right, 103 top, 103 bottom
Etienne Clément 83 bottom, 86 bottom, 87 top, 87 bottom right, 90 top, 91 centre left, 91 centre right, 91 bottom
Louis Hellman 86 top, 87 bottom left
Marianne Majerus 85 bottom left, 93 bottom, 94 top right, 95 bottom, 99 top left, 99 bottom, 106 top left, 107 top, 111 bottom, 112 top, 112 bottom left, 112 bottom right, 113 bottom
Sergison Bates 100 bottom, 101 top, 101 centre, 102 left
View 81 bottom
Walters and Cohen 80 top, 80 bottom, 81 centre
Barbara Weiss Architects 41 bottom, 82 top, 82 bottom, 83 centre, 84 bottom, 85 top, 85 bottom right, 88 top, 88 centre, 89 top left, 89 top right, 89 bottom, 90 bottom, 92, 93 top, 94 top left, 94 centre, 95 centre, 108 top right, 109 top, 109 bottom left, 109 bottom right, 110, 111 top, 113 top